# BECOMING
# <u>UN</u>STOPPABLE

# BECOMING
# UNSTOPPABLE

## TOOLS TO ELEVATE YOUR GAME

*Kristy B. Bidwill*

## KRISTY BIDWILL

Big Country Publishing

*"Kristy Bidwill's Unstoppable made me reevaluate how I want to live my life and what's holding me back from making my dreams my reality. I am inspired to try my own 90-day challenge and use Kristy's Nine Plays to map my course. A must read for everyone who wants to make changes to any part of their life."*
- Kiffie Robbins

*"I didn't know how lucky I was to have met Kristy Bidwill until after she unselfishly led me, a retired U.S. Army Captain and Blind Veteran, through every tedious and dangerous step to the summit of Mt. Kilimanjaro. As she reflects now on the nine plays she developed to Becoming Unstoppable, I continue to benefit from her inspiration and hope by sharing this formula for success that you, too, will see the transformational power of her methods. Once again, she has opened my blind eyes in this wonderful book."*
- Tom Hicks, Retired U.S. Army Captain and Blind Veteran

*"While coaching with Kristy, I learned the power of 'change for significance'. After navigating a devastating life change, I found new hope, new truth and a new love for my life! I now enjoy living life again operating in a peace and flow like never before!"*
- Rebekah Diaz, Founder & CEO The Action Foundation

*"Kristy's coaching was actually an answer to prayer when we first entered in this season. I saw a shift in many of my players and still hear them use the tools today. Personally, I learned some very valuable skills through our workouts and will never be the same!"*
- Chris Boehm, Tennis Professional

*Becoming Unstopppable-Tools to Elevate Your Game*
Copyright© 2014 by Kristy Bidwill
Library of Congress Control Number: 2014950957
ISBN: 978-1-938487-16-3
Cover Design: Rebekah Diaz
Cover Illustration: Jay David Clayton
Author Photography: Scott Foust

This memoir is a recollection of events to the best of the author's knowledge. Most details, including names, are real but some identities have been changed or are composites.

Published by
Big Country Publishing, LLC
7691 Shaffer Parkway, Suite C
Littleton, CO 80127
USA
www.bigcountrypublishing.com
Printed in the United States of America
International printing in the U.K. and Australia

# CONTENTS

# DEDICATION

*For my personal hero, Tom, who opened my eyes to see what more life had to offer.*

*And to the love of my life, my husband Tim, who showed unconditional support in making this book a reality.*

# ACKNOWLEDGMENTS

This book would not have been possible without the people in my life who helped guide me, shape me, inspire me and, at times, believed in me more than I believed in myself. That list is long and I'm grateful to all. Here are some that stand out:

Tom Hicks for showing me bravery, strength, determination, and the true meaning of living with a passion. You will always hold the place of hero in my heart.

Kevin Cherilla and Marc Ashton for your tireless leadership and dedication to our Mt. Kili team and the cause. To my very first running coach, Brett Schumacher - as my love for running evolved, so did our friendship. Frank Sole for teaching me to swim when I could barely walk and giving me the encouragement to later tackle Alcatraz and my first Ironman.

Brett Williams, Jack Smith, and Ron Cavage for your amazing coaching and support throughout my 90 Day Challenge to accomplish my goals. Jayson Harris, my training partner - thank you for believing in me even when I didn't give you much to work with.

Rebekah Diaz for encouraging me when I felt down and for your friendship - you have redefined the meaning of a starfish.

Kate in Costa Rica for introducing me to yoga and the power of tranquility. Nick Goodman for your amazing coaching and friendship through my second Ironman. And my entire training team for your friendship, advice, and allowing a girl to tag along on your training trips.

Thanks also to my editor Nancy Marriott of New Paradigm Writing and Editing Services and all those who read this manuscript and gave valuable input. And thank you to Christina Calisto Winslow and the staff of Big Country Publishing who all worked so tirelessly to help me produce a book that would tell my story and inspire others to become unstoppable.

A special thank you to my parents who raised me to be independent, confident, courageous, compassionate, and full of life. You have shown me a lifetime of unconditional love.

Above all, I want to say thank you to my husband, Tim, for believing in me, encouraging me, and loving me. Without your support, I'm not sure I would have made the final leap to my new career. Together we make a powerful team and have created a beautiful life that I cherish deeply.

And Kingston, you have definitely lived up to the saying, *A dog is a (wo)man's best friend*. You have seen me through it all and remained loyally by my side.

# PROLOGUE

I was 5 years old when I recall my world taking shape. It was at that defining moment in time, that I began to learn about choices and their consequences. I began to understand how the choices we make shape who we become and the beliefs we hold true. For each of us, this moment is different. For me, it was my parents' divorce.

The image I hold true in my mind is that of a sunny afternoon. My parents were having a tense conversation in the kitchen while I sat on the staircase, divided from them by only a half-wall. At this young age I do not recall comprehending anything other than an unhappy tone. It was clear to me my parents were not getting along.

Suddenly, my parents called me into the kitchen. At first I thought I would be scolded for eavesdropping, but quickly learned they wanted to talk to me about something far more life-changing. I remember climbing in and out of each of their laps as they did their best to explain divorce to me and what we as a family were about to encounter. I'm not sure I understood their words—I just remember tears. This was my first memory of tears and heartache.

The next memory I have is of my dad packing his bags. My mom sat cross-legged on the hallway floor, holding me down as the tears streamed down my face. Moments later my dad walked past us with his bags in hand, never to enter our house again, severing the family tie that had bound us together.

Today, recalling that moment as an adult, it is as though I am looking down from above on the pain of three individuals. I can feel the child's pain of confusion and uncertainty. I can see the pain my father felt, knowing that a decision had been made, and he was the one who had agreed to pack his bags and leave. How difficult it was to walk by his little girl and out of the house they had shared. And the pain my mother felt, having to hold on tightly to her crying little girl, also recognizing the decision that had been made and she was the one to stay at home with a 5 year-old child.

The months and years to follow definitely came with their fair share of difficulties. My parents' relationship would never be a friendly one, yet there was no question they both always had my best interest at heart. As heart-breaking as that defining moment of their separation was and will always be, I can also say my childhood was filled with happiness, laughter, and a lot of smiles. I learned at a young age that while my family may not live together under one roof, I was blessed with two amazing parents. I also learned at a young age how living with divorced parents meant I had two of everything: two bedrooms, two Thanksgivings, and, best of all, two Christmases.

As a teenager, I watched and learned from my parents, both of whom were extremely driven to succeed professionally. My father owned a business while my mother was a top executive in a large firm and later an executive director of a local nonprofit. They showed me firsthand the value of commitment, hard work, and professionalism. They encouraged me to pursue my interests and helped me build the confidence that I could accomplish anything I set my mind to.

I went to college with aspirations of becoming a doctor with a specialization in sports medicine. While registered for pre-med at Kansas State University, I had a professor who made one comment that forever changed my direction. He said, "If you have any doubts about medical school, don't go." He may very well have said more that day, but my mind got stuck on that one simple statement. Now looking back, I wonder what 19-year-old doesn't have doubts. Regardless, I took it to heart and after exploring numerous professions, settled on a business degree. Still uncertain, yet aiming to graduate with my friends, I thought a business degree made sense. It encapsulated what success looked like to me growing up and it was general enough to allow me the flexibility to figure out the specifics later.

Immediately after graduating I moved to Arizona to start my career with an advertising/public relations firm. Not even 30 days into my new job I questioned if I was cut out for business. This uncertainty led me to inquire about a teaching certification at Arizona State University with a goal that I could teach kindergarten. Just as I was about to apply for the program, I made a pitch to a local general contractor to provide public relations services. After a second meeting the contractor offered me a full-time position to lead their marketing and public relations efforts. I made the leap and soon found myself also running their business development efforts for their commercial division, responsible for bringing in new business.

After four incredible years I left the contracting business and was recruited into an international architecture, engineering, and planning firm to lead their business development division for the Southwest Region. By the age of 31 I had become the youngest, first non-technical, and only female partner in their Arizona office. The 17 years I spent in this industry led to numerous leadership opportunities, board presidency positions, a national speaking role, and notable recognition both within the industry and the community.

It was definitely a career full of accomplishments and one I am extremely proud to call mine. Yet throughout these years no matter how many awards and how much recognition I received, I always had a sense that there was something more for me in life. The questions never left me: Was this the career and life I really wanted? Or had I let my choices define me, choices that may have had more to do with what was expected of me than what in my heart I truly wanted?

On the personal side, I lived a very active lifestyle and was involved in sports from a young age. From the time I was born, the summers were spent at our lake house where my love for the water naturally evolved. Before I was even big enough to hold my own skis together my dad would position me on his skis while I held onto his legs. My younger years were also filled with dance, baton twirling, and competitive gymnastics. In high school I took up Tae Kwon Do, reaching the level of first-degree black belt, and brought home two gold medals at Junior Olympics.

Cheerleading became my sport of choice in high school and college. I cheered for varsity football and basketball, holding the position of team captain for both my senior year. In college, immediately after basketball season ended, our team competed in ESPN cheer competitions. I merged my love for children and the sport by choreographing and teaching summer cheer camps throughout those eight years.

After college I continued to look for ways to coach. However, with my career taking off, it became increasingly difficult to find the time. Looking for a new sport to fill the void, I took up running. It actually began more as a dare. A friend had made a New Year's resolution to run 1,000 miles that year and commented that I probably couldn't do it.

The gauntlet had been thrown. On January 1, 2000, I took to the roads and completed a 2-mile run around a nearby golf course. I thought my legs were going to collapse and my lungs explode. Knowing I needed to get in 20 miles a week to reach my goal, I ran doubles on a few days—2 miles in the morning and 2 miles at night—until slowly, I was able increase my mileage.

Nine weeks later I entered my first race, a half-marathon (13.1 miles). Prior to race day, 11 miles was the farthest I had ever run. Running was not something that came naturally to me yet I learned to put mind over matter and cross the finish line, a valuable lesson I looked back on time and time again.

In December of that same year I ran my first full marathon (26.2 miles). My love for running was born. The next month I hired a coach and joined a running group with the goal of qualifying for the Boston Marathon, which I did in a qualifying race later that year. Only 16 months after my first marathon, I traveled to Boston, completing my third marathon, a significant accomplishment for any person who had been running for such a short period. Over the next eight years, I ran seven more marathons and finished in two Ironman races.

Running became my outlet. It was my therapy. It gave me energy and clarity to handle the pressures of my career. Later it became my social outlet as my circle of running friends grew. I transformed from a night owl to an early bird in order to beat the Arizona heat and get my training miles in before my workday began. I was completely in my element and loved the escape it afforded. This was the time in my day when I felt completely authentic; doing something that had nothing to do with what was expected of me, just purely my heart's desire. And I loved it.

While my career was flourishing and running was fulfilling me, my personal life, however, was anything but remarkable. I seemed to have courage and confidence in every aspect of my life except the one area where I felt I had no control. I married at 27 despite my doubts. I then spent the next five years living a life that was not my own. I did my best to let everyone think I had the perfect marriage, the one only in my fantasies—but hid the reality. While I was being promoted to partner, my husband was suffering from depression and what I coined as alcohol abuse after two major layoffs. Our life together was full of disappointment, hurt, and frustration. I did everything I could think of to keep our marriage together—counseling, couple's Bible study, and prayer. Time after time, the relationship fell short of my expectations, and we grew further and further apart.

In 2006 I made the decision to divorce. It was the hardest decision I have ever made. The next six years I spent rediscovering me, the person I had slowly lost over my adult years. It was a time when all the questions in my life resurfaced and begged to be answered: Was I living the life I was meant to live, the life that most deeply fulfilled me personally and professionally? Who was I authentically and what was I put on this Earth to do—my purpose in life? What would be my legacy after my life was done—what difference will I have made?

These were the big questions that I tackled head-on. The answers came as I continued to meet challenges and leap beyond what I thought was possible and then meet new challenges, each time gaining a valuable lesson in finding my way—my truth. My authenticity. This book tells the story of my six-year journey of self-discovery and the tools I discovered that helped me to live a life of purpose, power, and authenticity in all that I do.

My hope is that the nine tools presented in this book—tools forged out of my own experience of success and failure, winning and losing, exhilaration and disappointment—will empower others to pursue their dreams beyond what they could ever imagine: *becoming unstoppable.*

# CHAPTER 1

# CHOOSING TO HOPE:
# A BACK-BREAKING ORDEAL

*Obstacles are what you see
when you take your eyes off your goal.*
—Jim Lefevre

The sunrise at 16,000 feet is very different than it is at sea level. There is no view of the sun rising over the horizon. Rather, the sky gradually begins to glow as though someone were slowly turning a dimmer switch to light up a dark room.

It's 7:00 a.m., just 3,000 feet short of the summit of Mt. Kilimanjaro, and the sky is now fully lit. I am part of a team that is guiding eight blind hikers to summit Africa's tallest mountain. We've reached a plateau known as Stella Point, where we are stopping briefly to rest, enjoy the view, and warm our freezing bodies with a cup of hot tea. Uhuru Peak, the true summit of Mt. Kilimanjaro, is still an hour away, and we are all very excited to make our final ascent after seven days on the mountain.

Reflecting back on how I'd gotten to this moment in my life, it was shocking to realize how I'd almost missed out on this adventure that I'd committed to through my work with The Foundation for Blind Children. It was only 10 weeks earlier when I awoke early one morning to discover that my dream to climb Mt. Kilimanjaro—and to take a blind hiker with me to the summit—was about to come crashing down.

As my eyes opened, all I could see was solid black. Rolling over, I caught a glimpse of a glow in the dark reading 4:30.

Reality hit. It was early Monday morning, and I had just been awakened by the sound of my alarm clock. Pulling my arm out from the warmth of the covers, my hand landed heavily on top of the clock, enough to stop the awful noise. In no time I was snuggled back onto the comfort of my pillow with my eyelids shut. Perhaps I could drift back to sleep and return to the dream from which I'd been so abruptly yanked.

I have no recollection of how much time had passed, but it couldn't have been very long. I only recall a jerk-like reaction that shot me out of bed with sheets and pillow flying. Kingston, my Rhodesian Ridgeback who occasionally slept in the bed with me, quickly followed.

It's Monday! I'm meeting a friend at 5:00 a.m. to run our 6-mile weekly "recovery" hill loop. I know, *recovery* and *hill* are two words that don't fit easily into the same sentence. But to my friend and me, both of us having run 15 miles the day before, any slower pace could be categorized as recovery.

Glancing at the clock, I was relieved to see it was only 4:40. I could still make it on time if I hurried. Rushing to grab my clothes laid at the foot of the bed, I noticed a shooting pain in the lower right side of my back. *Gosh darn it*, I thought. *It's still there.* I had noticed the pain the day before when coming off the longer run but had paid little attention to it.

*Oh well. One more run won't hurt anything. Anyway, I can't bail now, just a few minutes before the run,* I said to myself. If there is one unwritten code that any serious runner lives by, it is to never stand up your fellow running partner, especially if it's just the two of you. And never, ever when it's still dark outside.

My morning ritual always starts by getting into my running clothes. As I lifted my right leg up and my upper body bent over to step into my shorts, something seemed to catch. My foot did not quite make it into the leg hole. I should have known something was very wrong when the simple task of putting on a pair of running shorts required a thoughtful strategy. But who has time to second guess my plans for the day when a running date awaits?

Quickly throwing my hair into a ponytail and topping things off with a visor left me only time to stretch while brushing my teeth. *I'll be fine once I get moving,* was my reaffirming thought.

Kingston watched me dolefully, knowing he'd be cooped up for the day until I got home and could take him out for a short evening run on the trails behind our house.

It was only a 10-minute drive to our gym's parking lot, the starting point for our 6-mile run. With no time to spare, we exchanged brief hellos, knowing we'd have plenty of time to catch up on the run. Cars locked, Garmin watches on, we were off.

Monday morning runs always start with brief complaints of aches and pains coming off the longer Sunday runs. The purpose of the Monday run was mainly to get legs moving and flush out muscles of any lactic acid buildup. I kept my commentary to a minimum that day but did mention my need to get in to see my chiropractor for an adjustment and massage.

Conversation resumed as normal, catching up on the weekend's festivities and upcoming week's plans. For some reason that day, we took an unplanned detour for a water break behind the elementary school by the ball field. Getting back to the road that circled the school required climbing a few steps, perhaps a dozen. I noticed my back was stiff and a few quick shots of pain pulsed through my body. *Just another mile and half to go*, I told myself. *You can do anything for another 12 minutes.*

I will never forget the shooting pain I felt as I took the first step towards resuming my running pace. Tears filled my eyes. I tried hard to hide my misery and regain my composure. All I knew at that point was I wanted back to the car as quickly as possible. Logically, running was the fastest way.

I had to think of a way to minimize the effort it took to keep my legs propelling me forward. All I had to do was pick them up one at a time. *That's it. Pick 'em up and put 'em down,* I repeated to myself, evoking the mantra I'd used when I competed in the Boston Marathon to carry me through to the finish line.

To make our loop a full 6-miles we had to run a quarter mile past our cars and then turn around. Not wanting to let my friend down, I continued despite the pain. What was another quarter mile at this point? Perhaps in my mind I rationalized this as more running etiquette: once on a run, never let your running partner down by quitting.

Finally back at my car, I could breathe a sigh of relief. I had survived the run. After a short drive home, I would only have time to grab a quick shower before heading off to an early morning meeting. Regardless of my promise to make an appointment with my chiropractor, I had no time to spare. I could make the call between meetings later that morning.

As on any other morning after my run, I pulled into my garage and quickly gathered up my things to head inside for a shower. At a normal pace, I swung my legs out of the car and stepping down, began to stand. There was a sudden catch in my back, causing me to grab the car door to keep from falling over. A sharp paralyzing pain left me hunched over, unable to move. Just a normal exhale seemed to trigger sharper bouts of agony. I changed my breathing to long, slow, steady inhales and exhales which, if nothing else, calmed the wave of panic that was beginning to build. Ever so gently, I began to straighten out as much as I could bear. *Just a few more inches,* I thought to myself, *and I'll be able to shuffle my way into the house.* Such a simple task, but it felt like it took an eternity.

Mentally, I tried to minimize the pain. I told myself I must have just pinched my sciatic nerve, the large nerve that begins in the lower back and runs through the buttock and down the lower limb. This had happened before and it had eventually resolved itself. *The pain will pass…*

Only it didn't. Still hunched over, I braced myself on the car and inched forward. Once inside the house, I found whatever I could to hold on to all the way to the shower, stopping frequently to catch my breath from the pain. I told myself that if I could just get into the shower the hot water would loosen up whatever was causing this pain. With both hands I lifted the weight of one leg over the bathtub and then the other. Bracing myself up under the stream of hot water, I waited but relief never seemed to come. Something was very, very wrong.

I was not someone who visits the doctor frequently. In fact, I could not name my general practice physician, if I even had one. Other than having the annual strep throat as a child, I never got sick. At a young age my parents discovered I had a long list of allergies. As long as I visited my allergist and my ear, nose and throat specialist regularly, I was as healthy as anyone could ever hope to be.

But being an endurance athlete, I did have a chiropractor. This was mostly because I enjoyed the deep tissue massages from his in-house massage therapist. Occasionally I would find myself out of alignment but certainly never had any problem a simple adjustment could not correct. So instinctively, I called my chiropractor, Dr. Walters. It was still early and the office was not yet open. Having already spent my allotted time before work just trying to move around, I knew there was no way I could make it to downtown Phoenix in time for my business meeting. My next call had to be to my office to cancel my morning appointments.

My only objective at this point was to get ready for the day and hope my first stop would be at Dr. Walters' office. As I went into my closet to pick out something to wear, it occurred to me that I was going to have to alter my usual attire of high heels. But to a shoe lover, what else was there? The only pairs of flats I owned were flip-flops or boots. Spring in Arizona definitely meant boot season was over. Flip-flops it was. Far from intending to make a fashion statement I wore my professional clothing and my flips, but I didn't care.

By the time I was ready, hours had passed since my first stabbing pain, and it was now 9:00 a.m. Dr. Walters' office was open and they agreed to get me in immediately. Luckily his office is only another short 10-minute drive from my house, yet the effort spent walking to and from my car seemed to double the time. Little did I know my words, *I'll be right there,* would equate to 30 minutes.

It did not take Dr. Walters long to assess the situation and determine that my back was too inflamed for any kind of real examination. In fact, it was so inflamed that he could not feel the bone structure or muscles enough to even begin to make a diagnosis. Instead, he moved me into a room with a narrow examination table next to the TENS (*transcutaneous electric nerve stimulation*) machine, a fancy name for a device that produces electric currents for therapeutic purposes. The TENS sent electric pulses through four electrodes placed on my skin. The electric pulses are said to help reduce pain while the ice bags placed over the top reduce inflammation.

After 15 to 20 minutes on the machine Dr. Walters tried to examine the area again. To the best of his ability, he thought it was possibly a torn *piriformis*, a muscle that runs deep under the *gluteus maximus*, or butt cheek. But within minutes of being off the TENS, my back had tightened once again, making walking nearly impossible.

Dr. Walters gave me an anti-inflammatory pill and a mobile stimulation machine, which hung on my belt and sent constant electric pulses to my muscles, similar to the machine in his office. The constant electric pulse was an attempt to keep my muscles as relaxed as possible, allowing me the ability to at least move around, even if slowly. He also stressed the importance of icing frequently to keep the swelling down.

Unfortunately, I had a full day of meetings. Having already cancelled my morning, I could not fathom missing the rest of the day. Mid-afternoon I was scheduled to attend Opening Day of the Diamondbacks, Arizona's professional baseball team. While it may not sound like work to most, events like this were a key part of my job as the business development professional for my firm. A national construction firm in town was hosting me in their suite with the expectation of later discussing upcoming building opportunities. With the ballpark just a few blocks from my office, another partner from my firm and I planned to walk over together. Thinking that the pain stemmed from just a torn muscle, I could not justify canceling. Luckily my partner was very understanding and patient when my walking stride was reduced to mere inches at a time. When the pain got too bad, I had to stop momentarily to catch my breath. Somehow we were able to make it to the ballpark and up to the suite before the first pitch.

I got home that night and collapsed in bed. There was no run for Kingston that evening, but he seemed to understand. One look in his eyes and I could see he knew I was hurting. I let him up on the bed with me and tried to give him a cuddle, but all I could do was reach over and turn off the lights.

## STAYING THE COURSE

Survival of day one left me exhausted, but with a busy week ahead I had to stay the course. The next day I was scheduled for a business trip to Colorado, returning four days later on Friday afternoon in time for a fundraiser at a local museum to benefit The Foundation for Blind Children. I was on the board of directors for this organization and served as the chair of the Kilimanjaro Campaign, a year-long effort to fund a trip to Mt. Kilimanjaro where a group of 25, including eight blind students, would hike for eight days to reach the summit. The goal was to show the world that people living with visual impairment could accomplish anything a sighted person can, they may just approach things differently. The proceeds from our campaign would fund the Foundation's infant program, a program currently at risk due to state budget cuts. This museum event was one I had been intimately involved in planning and was our last big push for donors. Missing it was not an option.

I was given a few strict orders from Dr. Walters: first, wear the portable TENS machine daily and ice at least three times a day; and second, utilize the airport's wheelchair or motorized cart service, which at the time was Phoenix Sky Harbor

Airport's people mover system; and finally, I was to see him Friday afternoon, immediately after my plane landed and before my museum event.

The next four days were not pleasant. Every day I was in and out of the car attending meetings in Denver, and every night I spent in my hotel room icing my back. The pain was so great that by the end of the day, I would literally collapse on the bed with an ice pack and not get up until the next morning. I was in so much discomfort that I couldn't go out to restaurants or even stomach room service dinners.

One meeting in particular has remained a vivid memory to this day. It was my first time visiting a prominent Colorado architectural firm in which I was exploring a partnership with my company. After a brief tour of the office, I found myself at the base of a spiral staircase leading to their second floor loft where my meeting with several of their partners would be held. In a matter of a few seconds two thoughts made their way through my head. The first was, *There is no way I can get up those stairs!* Next, *You have to!* With pride swallowed, I took a big breath and let out a quiet sigh with each step.

By Friday mid-morning, I was on my way back to the Denver airport. Not having heeded Dr. Walters' advice to utilize the people mover at Sky Harbor when coming, I now reconsidered. While I historically viewed these modes of transportation as reserved for the disabled, I was willing to entertain the thought that I now qualified. As luck would have it, I could not find one that day. How many times have I been nearly run over in airports by a wheelchair or a people mover? Yet today, there was not a single one in sight.

Despite the five days of pain, seeing Dr. Walters Friday afternoon was somewhat uplifting. He was as encouraging as possible. He admitted the inflammation had worsened but assured me it was only because I had not yet let my body rest. It was only to be expected after flying at high altitudes and the amount of activity I did each day, just getting around from one meeting to the next. Once I had gotten through that night's fundraiser, I planned to rest for the remainder of the weekend. He assured me with two days of rest, continued use of the TENS machine and ice, I would feel relief by Monday.

## MONDAY'S VISIT

Walking into Dr. Walters' office Monday morning was a slow and painful process. He took one look at me hobbling through the waiting room and knew there was something far worse going on than he'd first thought. We did not even make it to the exam room before he explained that if I had a purely muscular injury, I would have relief by now. No examination was required for him to see this was not the case. He wanted an MRI. Knowing that I would be departing for Kilimanjaro in only nine weeks, he urged me to get on the schedule for the following day.

Not expecting to hear my results for at least 24 hours, I was surprised when my cell phone rang Wednesday morning as I was on my way into my office. It was Dr. Walters. He did not waste any time asking how I was feeling; instead he led with, "I have good and bad news." The MRI results showed I had a fracture in my *sacrum*, the large, triangular bone at the base of the spine that forms the pelvic cavity. A fracture at that part of my back was not something he'd previously even considered, since such a break would normally be the result of a major fall, such as from a bucking horse. I assured him that I hadn't done any horseback riding lately.

Finding the positive side, Dr. Walters told me that sacrum fractures typically take eight to 10 weeks to heal, leaving me just enough time to heal before I was scheduled to set foot at the base of Mt. Kilimanjaro. He assured me it was possible for me to completely heal in enough time, and he was committed to do everything possible to make it happen. He had already consulted a few of his colleagues and wanted to start treatment immediately. Without hesitation, I turned the car around and went straight to his office.

The body is an amazing machine with its own built-in defensive mechanisms. When the body experiences a trauma, the muscles surrounding the trauma tighten to provide protection to the injured area. For this reason, Dr. Walters shared my MRI results with his massage therapist, so she could understand which muscles to concentrate on and loosen up in her treatments. Massage therapy three times a week to relax the muscles and break up the scar tissue surrounding the sacrum break became my ritual.

At home, I applied cold and warm herbal compresses and took a variety of vitamins, all with the intention of stimulating cell rejuvenation. I was advised that rest and time is the best prescription for a fracture.

Some do believe in the power of natural herbs and vitamins. Wanting to do whatever possible, I included all recommended supplements in my treatment plan.

Regardless of my confidence in Dr. Walters' treatment, I sought a second opinion and the advice of a well-known sport and spine specialist in town. Knowing full well I was going to summit Kilimanjaro, I wanted to be sure that I was doing everything possible for the quickest recovery. Reviewing the results of my MRI, the specialist was surprised at the severity of my fracture. Despite the background I provided, he questioned how this had happened, asking me twice if I had not experienced some kind of a fall. He was also surprised I had not yet taken any medication for the pain, not even as much as ibuprofen. At this point, I was two weeks from the actual fracture and a week past my MRI. I am not sure if the pain had lessened or I had just become accustomed to it. Either way, the specialist's diagnosis concurred with that of Dr. Walters. The only thing he added in treatment was a prescription for *Vicodin*, a painkiller used to relieve moderate to severe pain. I never filled the prescription.

## THE HEALING PROCESS

Week two brought with it a new set of challenges and emotions. The newness of my situation had worn off, and I now faced the reality of functioning in my daily life with a back fracture. Sure, there was the increased difficulty getting around and the triggers of pain from simply carrying a bag of groceries, but for those chores I learned to plan extra time. However, the greatest emotional blow came from the reduction in the amount time I was able to be physically active.

Because of my sacrum fracture I was forced to take a break from my daily workouts which included the activity I loved the most, running. On the one hand, since I could barely walk, it was not hard to skip my morning runs. The pain was so great, I would just pray to be able to move around my house and at work pain-free. On the other hand, I felt a tremendous mental, physical, and emotional loss.

When your primary outlet is physical activity, taking that away brings about an array of consequences. Not only did my mind and body miss the endorphin high, I began to deteriorate psychologically. I would describe it as a kind of mini-depression. Running served as far more than simply exercise for me. Running with friends was my social life, it was therapeutic, and also just plain fun. It was a way for me to relieve stress, work through problems, and come up with new ideas. It was a way for me to start every day on a positive note which, I believe enabled me to handle the stresses of my job and all of life's ups and downs with an optimistic attitude. Without that release I felt as though my life were slowly beginning to crumble.

Just like anyone, I had my fair share of disappointments and hardships in life. However, I always seemed to have the ability to take things in stride. Now it wasn't so easy. I went through the typical stages of loss. First there was denial: *It is just a torn muscle*. And then there is bargaining: *Just make it go away*, I would pray. Then came the anger. *Why is this happening to me?* I had commitments. I had the Kilimanjaro hike for which I'd already invested nearly a year of training time. I had a home and dog to care for and, selfishly, I had my cherished routine of running. The hardest stage was despair: the tears that filled my eyes when I drove past runners, the moments of lost hope that fluttered through my thoughts. *I'll never heal in enough time to reach the summit*, I thought.

But eventually the despair passed, and I was able to come to acceptance. I could not feel sorry for myself any longer. In the game of life we are dealt many hands. Some of the plays are obvious, but others take time to figure out. Nothing can happen until we play the next card. Week two of my back-breaking ordeal marked the time for me to play the next card. I was ready to accept the adversity life had put in my path and chose to meet it from a place of hope.

## FINDING NEW HOPE

By the second week out from my diagnosis I was on the other side of my ordeal, and swimming had become my answer. Well, at least I was going to give it my best shot.

I was not a swimmer. As I mentioned earlier, I spent a great deal of time as a child waterskiing and most of my summer days playing in a pool. But I would not call myself a swimmer. After all, I wore a life vest in the water and only had to swim short distances. My summer days in the pool looked more like jumping off a diving board, playing Marco Polo, and performing water ballet routines than swimming laps. While I may not have been afraid of the water, I was definitely not blessed with any natural swim stroke skills. I had a few formal swim lessons, but swimming laps in a pool was much less interesting than waterskiing on a lake.

I soon learned that my understanding of a swim stroke was far from text book, and learning to pace my breathing in the water seemed like an entirely new concept. As a marathon runner, I breathed whenever I wanted to. As a swimmer, every breath is timed and evenly released. I found myself out of breath just swimming the length of the pool—a 25-meter pool at that!

My newfound love for the water grew out of daily 15-minute swims using a pull buoy. This is a floatation device placed between a swimmer's thighs, eliminating the need to kick. Swimmers use pull buoys so they can focus on their upper body technique while keeping their lower body afloat. I used it to drag my lower body along, since I was not yet allowed to kick.

It did not take long to discover that the water was the only place I had relief from the consistent pain. It was magical! I began to crave my time in the water. I found myself in the pool at my fitness club twice a day, early before work and immediately after my workday ended. This was still a far cry from the amount of daily activity I had grown accustomed to as a runner. Yet for those 15 minutes I was nearly pain free and I was getting my body moving.

After a few weeks of these short swims Dr. Walters instructed me to stand in the water at the side of the pool and do leg raises to the front and the back, not yet to the side. He wanted me to begin working on my range of motion in a weightless environment.

Once I received my doctor's clearance, I sought the instruction of a Masters Swim coach, Frank Sole. In Masters Swimming classes, coaches write workouts and provide feedback and instruction for people wanting to improve their swimming ability. Frank began teaching me proper stroke techniques through swim drills, ultimately increasing my time in the water. At this point my swimming was still all upper body, utilizing the assistance of the pull buoy. But my love for swimming was born.

In addition to swimming I focused my attention on working with Tom Hicks in my commitment to guide him up to the summit of Mt. Kilimanjaro. Tom Hicks is a blind Army veteran whom I had been paired with for the Kilimanjaro climb. Together with another sighted guide, Grahame, we formed the three-person Team Hicks and joined a larger group of 25 climbers total. Not only had my eyes become Tom's vehicle to hike, Tom had become my responsibility and my friend. I was not about to let Tom, my team, the group, or myself down.

The team's monthly hikes were now happening every other week. The distances began to increase as well as the weight each member carried in his or her pack. Still very much a part of the team, I attended the team hikes but sat in the parking lot handing out fliers to promote our adventure and ask for donations. As the group would disappear up the trail of the mountain, so would my connection to my team. Another hiker from another team was taking my place guiding Tom. Someone else was learning those final details in guiding techniques that I would need to know and have mastered in just a few short weeks. This caused me a bit of anxiety. But soon after the team was out of sight, it was like a rubber band snapped and I had to bring myself back into reality. I had to remember what was most important, which was to represent The Foundation for Blind Children, to increase awareness for the visually impaired, and raise money for the Foundation's programs. My back may have been broken but the rest of me was not. I sat in a folding chair with my fliers and struck up a conversation with anyone who came within earshot of our SUV.

I focused on doing my part to get healthy as quickly as I could, which included listening to Dr. Walters' orders, never missing my massage treatments, alternating hot and cold herbal compress treatments, and taking my daily dose of vitamins. With the exception of my workouts, the rest of my life remained intact. I still met the demands of my position as partner of my firm, I still kept up my household chores and cared for Kingston, and I still maintained my personal relationships. Everything in my day just took a little more time to do. I learned to schedule more time between my business meetings, even those that took place internally within my company. Just walking down the hall, to and from my car, and running short errands took more time than before.

I even adjusted to having what I called my "couch time." Before my fracture, I rarely, if ever, sat idly on the couch. I was always active, up and about in my spare time. For that reason, when my doctor suggested I do my hot and cold compresses while watching TV, my reply was, *I don't watch TV.* In fact, the television I owned was a 19-inch box I had bought in 1996, 10 years prior. I also did not have a cable subscription, so the number of available channels was rather limited. Living in Greater Phoenix, I actually got more

Spanish-speaking channels than English. So for my couch time with the compresses, instead of watching TV, I would tend to emails, complete work I didn't get done in the office, or take a few minutes to catch up with my friends on the phone since I no longer had my morning runs for socializing.

Just a few weeks before the group was to depart for Africa, I was able to resume my role as a full team member on hikes, although I didn't yet feel strong enough to add the weight of a pack. Daypacks fit tightly around the waist, distributing most of the weight onto the hips, the central core of the body. My first day carrying a daypack would be Day One on Mt. Kilimanjaro.

## MOVING THROUGH ADVERSITY

I've shared my story not from a need for sympathy, but rather from the desire to demonstrate what I've learned about facing adversity with hope. Going through sadness and disappointment when you've had an injury or loss is natural. However, it is only a healthy process if you find your way beyond your grieving to the phase of acceptance.

While there is no set time for the grieving process, or for moving between the phases—each person is unique—being stuck in denial, bargaining, anger, or despair without ever coming to acceptance only leads to resentment and bitterness.

Acceptance is the phase where a door can open and a shift can occur. That's what happened to me when I finally got over my despair and self-pity. Everyone has the ability to change their mindset and shift directions in light of a new hope—and it's hope that provides motivation.

I grew up believing I could accomplish anything I set my mind to. I believed that all I had to do was create a plan, follow the plan, and my goal would be met, exactly how I envisioned it. While I knew my life had never played out this way in reality, for some reason I clung to my belief in this idealistic, fairytale world.

My back-breaking experience showed me just how unrealistic and naive my thinking had been. Here was an obstacle the size of which I'd never before encountered, and it required of me a whole new way of thinking. Faced with my back-breaking ordeal, I realized I had two choices. I could put everything on hold, feel sorry for myself, and wait for some resolution to magically occur. Or I could figure out a way to survive and flourish. I chose the second. If you hadn't guessed, I am not very good at waiting.

## PLAYBOOK

### Play #1: Choose to Meet Adversity with New Hope

When dealing with any adverse condition, unfortunate circumstance, or events in your life, you can always make a choice that will determine the outcome. First, you can choose how you view the situation. Is it a complete game changer or rather something that is simply in your way? Secondly, you can choose how you are going to react to the situation and, as a result, the action you are going to take. Are you going to give up? Or will you search for new hope to create a new possible future?

Picture a lightbulb. When the light is turned on, your vision is clear. You can see where you want to go and can see the obstacles that may stand in your way. You have the vision to react to anything standing in your way of reaching your destination. However, when the lightbulb is turned off you are left standing in the dark. Your vision has been blocked. You can no longer see where you want to go, nor can you see your surroundings. Even if you know the general direction of your destination, you may bump into obstacles along the way. If you trip and fall, how will you react? Will you sit and wait to be rescued? Or will you find another way to continue toward your destination?

When you are faced with adversity in life, it is as though you have turned off the lights and have been left standing in the dark. While you may still know the general direction of where you want to go, it is no longer easy to navigate the path.

Choosing to view the situation positively by creating new hope prevents you from getting stopped and turns on the lightbulb. In the light you can choose further how you want to react to what life has dealt you. Do you still want to reach the same destination? Or would you prefer to establish a new goal? Either way, something has changed, and so must you. You have either declared a new goal, in which case you must develop a new game plan, or the path to reach your original destination now looks completely different, requiring a new course of action.

Any time you are faced with change you can bring new hope to your circumstances and from there move toward your goal, whatever it may be. New hope often comes from you connecting to a person or a community that can provide the support and encouragement you need in order to reach your goal. This person or community becomes your lifeline to call upon.

At times it may feel as though the people supporting you believe in you more than you believe in yourself. They encourage and motivate you when you feel deflated. They listen and comfort you, yet hold you accountable when you are not true to your words. They remind you of the obstacles you have already overcome and build confidence for those not yet tackled. They provide you new hope, and it is the new hope that you have chosen.

# Kristy's Game Time Coaching
# Journal Entry

What kinds of adversity have you met in your life? An injury, the loss of someone close, a radical change in something you could not control, such as your finances, your home and location, your choice of a mate—all of these can be obstacles in your course and throw you off your original intentions or goals. Were you able to come away from those events with a new hope that led to a new path? If so, how did you arrive at your new hope? What choices did you make that caused a turnaround, a victory?

If you are in the midst of such adversity now, what is its nature and what actions can you take that would bring about new hope? Can you choose to see the situation in a new way and then act to bring about your desired goal? Consider not only actions but also who you can turn to for support. Where will you find your inspiration to become unstoppable?

# CHAPTER 2

# DISCOVERING MY PURPOSE: MT. KILIMANJARO

*Find your passion and make it happen. Be on a mission and live your life on purpose. Be motivated by your desire to achieve rather than your fear of failure.*
—Unknown

The day had finally come. Everything we had done to prepare ourselves for the mountain was either going to carry us to the top or come tumbling down with us. My back was as healed as much as it was going to be and the rest of the group was in peak condition.

Our bags were packed with only the bare essentials, checked twice, and carefully weighed. We were given strict guidelines of specific items to pack, as our bags were to be weighed at the base of the mountain. Each one must pass a weight inspection before being carried up by Sherpas. The Sherpas played a significant role in our journey as they carried everything except our personal daypacks, prepared our meals, and set our tents ahead of our arrival each day.

Our personal daypacks that we carried included two 1-liter reusable water bottles, snacks, and additional clothing needed for the temperature swings. We were advised as to how much would be safe and realistic to carry for six plus hours a day, eight days straight.

It was time to board our flight to Detroit, the first leg of our 24-hour trip that would take us through Amsterdam and on to Africa to face our mountain. Standing at 19,340 feet and located in Tanzania, not far from the equator, Mt. Kilimanjaro is Africa's highest mountain and the closest point on the planet to the sun. The country of Tanzania is located in southeast Africa, its eastern border formed by the Indian Ocean. Mt. Kilimanjaro is located in the northeastern region of Tanzania.

This would be the mountain that, once conquered, would prove to the world that a person with visual impairments could achieve any task they set their mind to, just as a sighted person can. Little did I realize when boarding the flight that this adventure would also mark the beginning of my own personal life transformation. It was through this experience, including the year of training on weekends, my recuperation from a broken back, and the eight days on the mountain, that my life would take on new meaning and purpose, and I would be forever changed.

## TURNING POINT

At this point in my life I found challenges of all kinds to be personally fulfilling and had set my share of goals to reach, mostly in the area of sports and athletics. If I met my goal, such as setting a new marathon personal best, I would celebrate the new accomplishment and quickly move on to the next challenge. If I failed, I would criticize my shortcomings, never cutting myself any slack. I tended to be very hard on myself, a way of thinking that caused me to drive myself mercilessly, often to the point of not paying attention to my body's needs or any other needs I might have.

But something happened somewhere along the side of that mountain in Africa that would change everything. While I was well aware of my need for change prior to my trip, it was the eight days on the mountain that did the trick. It was as though I found new meaning to life and allowed the mountain to transform me. I went up as one person, and came down as someone new.

With my appetite for challenges, just as one adventure was complete, I would challenge myself to something new. It almost became a joke. The first question most of my friends would ask when they saw me was, *What are you training for next?* What I was about to learn was just how self-centered each of my goals had been, leaving me stuck in a perpetual cycle of seeking new challenges or regretting my failures. The continent that sat on the other end of our long flight was about to give me new motivation, one grounded in a sense of purpose and passion that stretched me so I would become unstoppable.

Mt. Kilimanjaro was a turning point for me. I had no idea how many life-altering lessons I was about to encounter in the coming years after conquering the mountain. The years that followed were some of the most amazing and truly fulfilling years of my life but, at the same time, brought about some of my life's most disappointing experiences. As it turns out, many of the shifts I have made in life have come as a direct result of the failures.

I would have plenty of opportunity in the coming years to practice turning around adversity with new hope. Never wanting to repeat hardships, I took them to heart and strived to learn from each one. However, there were times I thought I had it all figured out, only to discover the downfall was harder than I had experienced before. I would learn that there are more components to becoming unstoppable than lessons learned healing a broken back and summiting a mountain in Africa.

## HOW IT ALL BEGAN

Looking back, I just happened to be at the right place at the right time. I was attending a fundraising reception for The Foundation for Blind Children when I met Kevin Cherilla, a physical education teacher by training and an expedition leader by passion. At this point, Kevin had summited Kilimanjaro seven times and was one of the few to have successfully stood on the summit of Mt. Everest. Kevin shares his love for the mountains by guiding groups to the top of Kilimanjaro every summer.

That night our conversation quickly moved from simple introductions to hearing about a recent conversation Kevin had with Marc Ashton, the Foundation's Executive Director. Kevin and Marc had half-heartedly kicked around the idea of the two of them leading a few blind students to the summit of Mt. Kilimanjaro.

"It's just an idea, but we thought it would be a great way to raise money and awareness for the Foundation," Kevin said. As he spoke, I could see his enthusiasm grow. "We'd need some help coordinating the trip, and also a few people who'd be willing to act as guides for the visually impaired hikers on the mountain." He paused, noticing that he had my full attention. "Would you be interested if we ever made it happen?" he asked me.

Without blinking an eye, I said, "Yes."

I clearly remember driving home that night wondering where Mt. Kilimanjaro was and how high the mountain stood. Having grown up in the flatlands of Kansas, my perception of high might be a little skewed. Now living in Arizona, my perception of mountains was represented by Camelback Mountain and Piestewa Peak. Only standing 2,700 feet, these two would be considered by most to be mere foothills.

I had hiked these foothills several times since moving to the area in 1996, but I was far from a mountain climber, or even hiker, for that matter. Nor was I what you would call an outdoorsy person. I had actually never camped a single day in my life. My outdoor activities were limited to my early morning runs. I much preferred the rest of my activities to be the kind with indoor plumbing.

Despite my lack of outdoor skills, I was in fairly good physical shape. By this point in my life, I had run nine marathons and countless shorter races. My hobbies included waterskiing, wakeboarding, and lifting weights. In my younger years, I was a competitive gymnast, ballerina, high school and college cheerleader, and a first-degree, two-time Junior Olympic black belt in Tae Kwon Do. I did enjoy a healthy and active lifestyle.

As the conversation with Kevin and the idea he'd mentioned drew closer to becoming reality, so did my realization of just what I'd agreed to do. I was about to take on a strenuous, eight-day trek in freezing temperatures with no showers or indoor plumbing, and lead a blind person to the highest point on the African continent.

*What was I thinking?*

Perhaps it was sheer ignorance of what lay ahead, but I had to admit the idea of taking on such a gigantic challenge lifted me to exhilarating new heights. Climbing one of the seven highest summits of the world—just the thought of it made me smile from ear to ear.

The original offer was formalized as Kevin and Marc put their expedition and fundraising campaign together. But from the moment I had first accepted this offer, I knew climbing Kili would have a tremendous impact on my life. Initially, I accepted the offer for completely selfish reasons. It sounded like a once-in-a-lifetime adventure that I just could not pass up.

But that was before I had met Tom Hicks.

Tom is a hero to many and will certainly always hold that place in my heart. Tom was not born blind, he lost his sight as a young adult. Having spent so much time around various individuals with vision loss and hearing their stories, I often wonder if I had to choose, which would be better: to never have sight in the first place, or know what life is like with sight and suddenly have it taken away? Honestly, I absolutely cannot imagine either.

Tom wrote a letter at the beginning of our adventure that says it all. He was addressing potential donors at the outset of our campaign, *See Kili Our Way*, to raise money and awareness. Nothing beats Tom's own words. Here is an excerpt from that letter that gives a glimpse into the kind of person he is and why he is my personal hero:

April 27, 2009

My name is Thomas Hicks and I am 42 years old. I reside in Gilbert, Arizona, with my family. I am the father of seven wonderful children. Twelve years ago, I lost my eyesight serving in the U. S. Army to a progressive eye disease called *retinitis pigmentosa* (RP). It was nothing heroic that caused my blindness.

After 13 years serving both as an enlisted Military Policeman and a commissioned Military Intelligence Officer, my career came to a sudden and abrupt end when I first heard from an Army Ophthalmologist, "Captain Hicks, you are blind."

This news rocked my world and devastated my family. It was an unacceptable reality and we were overcome with fear and uncertainty. My first thought was, *How am I going to support my wife and children*? My second thought was, *No way am I going blind*! But no matter how hard I tried to deny the unacceptable reality of blindness, it was happening and all I could do was "suck it up" and prepare for this new life.

In the Army, I was forever challenging and pushing myself to become the very best soldier I could be. I was so proud to wear our country's armed forces uniform, and I could not imagine myself not serving anymore.

*Tom, the face of determination...my hero*

My last duty assignment was with the 1st Special Forces Group, Airborne at Fort Lewis, Washington, where I served as the Group's Signal Intelligence Officer. It was a dream assignment for a young Intelligence Officer and an opportunity that I would never fully realize because of blindness. I felt ashamed and embarrassed as I stood before my commander not fully capable of performing my job as he expected. My commander was compassionate and he allowed me to continue serving in the Group to the best of my capacity while I prepared for the medical board process. He did not have to do this and could have sent me directly to a medical hold company, filling my slot with an officer fit for duty.

For the first time in my adult life I was unable to drive, recognize faces, rank, or read name tags. One day in the Group's Headquarters building, I ran into my commander and knocked him down. I quickly apologized over and over to him as I helped him up off the floor. He was mad until he realized it was me. I was so embarrassed, but that's what blindness does to a person in the beginning. It didn't just take my eyesight. Blindness took my career, self esteem, self worth, and all of my independence.

On November 19, 1997, I was medically retired and processed out of the U. S. Army. The difficult transition to civilian life was compounded by the onset of my blindness. I just did not know where to turn or where I fit in. In the beginning, I felt all alone on this new journey. In the past 12 years, I have mobilized every possible state, federal, and community resource to help me with my adjustment. I needed to learn blind skills to improve my personal safety, independence, and overall quality of life. I wanted to keep working and I wanted to be a good example to my children. I would tell myself over and over, "You can't quit or give up Tom!"

Thomas L. Hicks, Captain, U.S. Army (Retired)

As the planning phase began, my role evolved from participant to the Board Liaison and then to Chair of the fundraising campaign that was connected with the trip. During the period of our training each team was asked to raise $15,000 for the Foundation through pledges, a task we gladly took on. Like our team, the other teams were comprised of two sighted guides and one blind student who had received educational services from the Foundation. Each team had committed to raising the $15,000. There were eight teams total, thus eight blind hikers who would train to make the summit attempt in June. Two of the blind hikers were teens and three were between 18 and 25. The adults, including the sighted guides, ranged from 25-44. In addition, we had a sighted 55-year-old guide who was also our team doctor accompany us up the mountain.

Our goals were defined in three parts. The first part was to create experiences for eight blind students. Second, we wanted to raise money for the Foundation. And finally, we sought to raise awareness of visual impairments and prove to the world that those affected can achieve anything. In the end, we accomplished all three. The eight blind students set four world records: the largest blind group to reach the summit of Kilimanjaro, the youngest person to summit, the first blind veteran, and the first person with albinism to summit. We raised more than $250,000 for the Foundation and saved the infant program from possible closure due to state budget cuts. And we made both local and national news, including NBC's Nightly News with Brian Williams.

We far exceeded all of our initial expectations. Yet those are only the tangible results of our efforts. There is another dimension that I am not sure anyone could have predicted: The lasting impressions made on the 25 individuals who experienced the adventure firsthand. For me, the impact was huge. Just thinking back to those days I feel a chill running up my spine.

## OUR ARRIVAL

We arrived at Kilimanjaro International Airport on a Sunday night at 7:45 local time. We were greeted by Nixon, our African lead guide, and his crew, a group Kevin had hired to help take us to the summit. The crew loaded our bags onto the tops of two old buses that looked so well-used, I questioned their ability to get us to our lodge. I do not recall the exact length of our ride. Perhaps I was too tired after reaching the end of a 24-hour travel period—although I do remember thinking we could not get to our lodge fast enough.

The only portion of our ride I can still envision was the final stretch. I recall thinking the landscape was lush but there was not much around in terms of building development. The road was bumpy and narrow, the last quarter mile leading into the resort unpaved. Once inside the lodge's gates, the property turned into a well-manicured village of modernized yet authentic huts. The main building was sizable with a lobby and shops which led to a large open-air restaurant overlooking a pool.

I was taken to my room on the second floor of one of the huts. My room was a suite; a living room and a bedroom connected by a hallway and divided by a bathroom. Outside the living room door, a balcony overlooked an amazingly lush creek surrounded by a jungle-like landscape. In the bedroom, a large net hung from the ceiling to enclose the king-sized bed and keep out insects. It was exactly how I'd envisioned Africa to be.

I took a quick shower, unpacked a few of my things and then joined the team for dinner in the restaurant. I did not crawl into bed until 2:00 a.m. but quickly fell sound asleep.

There was one full day before we were to begin our climb, and Kevin had arranged a community service day for us at the Mwereni School for the Blind. The next morning we loaded the buses once again to make the 45-minute drive into Moshi, where the school was located. I was not prepared for what awaited us inside the school gates. Hundreds of children ages 5 to 18 lined the driveway singing African songs and clapping as we drove in. As our buses stopped, the children circled around. Their faces looked so happy. I cannot recall a more welcoming arrival. I felt chills go up and down my spine.

The Mwereni School had a total enrollment of more than 600 students as well as housing 60 blind children under the age of 16. The school also served as protection for Tanzania's albino children who have been kidnapped and murdered for their body parts, a growing problem in the area. Many of the children the school serves are also orphans.

*Me with the Mwereni Kids*

Our day began with a tour. The most memorable part was the boys' dorms. The building was a simple concrete structure with a center hallway and rooms flanking each side. Each room was approximately 9' x 9' with two sets of bunk beds that slept eight boys, two boys sharing one twin-sized mattress. Their belongings were kept in a small trunk at the foot of the bed. They all shared a single restroom which consisted of a hole in the ground serving as the toilet and a single showerhead that provided some water for quick showers. I definitely saw a need for new dorms to be built.

After the tour we gathered in the multi-purpose room that was crowded with school children who were squeezed into tight rows of narrow tables and chairs. This is the moment we presented our donation of white walking canes and braillewriters for the blind students in the school. In return, they performed a series of song and dance presentations to the sound of drums. The room was filled with happiness and joy. These children lived simply yet celebrated richly.

We ended our day playing soccer with the children before we had to load the buses to make the drive back to our lodge. The children once again lined the driveway as we departed, leaving us with the sound of African song. I was so moved by what I'd experienced that day, it was hard for me to shift my focus towards our journey up the mountain that was to begin the very next morning.

## Ascent: Day One

The air was moist with a slight chill the day we pushed out from the base of the mountain at 6,200 feet. Back home my life was orderly and predictable. I was a partner of a large national architecture and engineering firm, and I had a rapidly growing career. Here on the side of Mt. Kilimanjaro I was just one of many, all trying to reach the summit. Back home I balanced the demands of my job with my early morning runs and took advantage of my company's great benefits package to travel internationally once per year. I had been to Australia, New Zealand, France, Germany, Austria, Mexico, and Belize, to name a few countries.

I would say my life was pretty good, yet for some reason I always felt like I needed something more. Over the years, I was able to satisfy those cravings through my marathons and travel adventures. I was always involved in some activity outside of my work hours that would stretch me beyond what I thought possible. But today none of my past accomplishments mattered. I was just another hiker trying to survive the mountain. Only I had the added responsibility of being Tom's eyes, so that he, too, could experience —and survive—the increasingly thin air as we gained altitude.

In single-file fashion, we began our rapid ascent along the Machame Trail which took us first through a spectacular rain forest. Its beauty was something out of a fairy tale, with 60-plus foot Rosewood trees scaling the mountainside, their dark green vines draped between them to make canopies that provided shade in the heat. The sound of howling monkeys and whistling birds echoed through the valleys. Three hours into our day's hike, our Sherpas surprised us with a quaint lunch break set up just off the trail. Just the sight of the sandwiches and fresh fruit had our group energized and full of smiles. After we ate we had no shortage of laughter and chatter as we continued our way up the trail.

*Me guiding Tom through the Rain Forest*

We reached the tree line at 9,937 feet and came upon a small opening which would be home to our first campsite. Having hiked ahead, the Sherpas already had our tents pitched for the night and a dinner consisting of cucumber soup, spaghetti, and white potatoes cooking—not exactly ideal for those of us accustomed to a low-carb diet. However, foods rich in carbohydrates were exactly what our bodies needed after nearly six hours of hiking.

This first night proved to be interesting in many ways. For one it was my first camping experience. And much to my dislike, the ground was damp and the air temperature had dropped rapidly. By the time I crawled into my tent, the air was downright bone chilling. I could not stop myself from worrying. How was I going to survive at much higher altitudes if I was already shivering at this first stop?

The campsite was so small that the tent lines were overlapping one another. Moving around, I felt like I was in a challenging obstacle course. I had to be careful not to trip over the crossing tent lines, especially in the pitch black of night. This left the blind hikers no option but to travel with an escort anywhere in the campsite.

As the night's temperatures continued to drop, I had to add more and more layers of clothing to stay warm. Even though the night was young, it wasn't difficult to convince me that it was time to cozy up in my sleeping bag. Still cold once inside it, I wrapped an extra fleece jacket around my already double-beanie layered head. No surprise, I had a difficult time falling asleep and even when I did, staying asleep wasn't any easier.

Our tent was on an ever-so-slight slope. I awoke to feel my feet pressing into the wall of the tent, as well as a full-on brain freeze as though I had just swallowed a big chunk of popsicle. My sleeping bag had slid to the bottom of the tent and my head was out of my warm triple layer wrap. I rolled groggily onto my stomach and did the bunny hop to get my bag back to the top. In complete darkness, I searched for my beanies and rewrapped the fleece around my head. This went on repeatedly throughout the night, causing me to wake up just about every hour. My tentmate, Grahame, and I later referred to this experience as the "slip-n-slide." Little did I know it would happen every night for the next six, despite our prayers for a campsite with a flat tent landing.

Oh, but the nightly entertainment did not stop there. Without the white noise of air conditioning, fans, traffic, or even the rustle of creatures, it was so quiet you could hear a pin drop. Those of us on the trip had a little joke that the nights were filled with the sound of music—the perfect harmony of snoring and flatulence.

This first night, Tom's tent was next to ours. It became apparent he experienced the same trouble sleeping as I did. Just about every hour, I could hear him check his watch for the time. Since he obviously could not see, he had one that spoke to him every time he checked it, and it was not in a whisper. *It is 2:15 AM*. Not long after, *It is 3:45 AM*.

## DAY TWO

The next morning proved that there is definitely such a thing as waking up on the wrong side of the tent. At breakfast I was irritable from the lack of sleep and didn't want a repeat of my previous night's disturbances. I was quick to point out to Tom that if he did not want to hear me say, *Oh sorry, I didn't see that rock*, he might consider limiting just how often he checked the time on his watch tonight. We both got a good laugh, but I believe he got my point.

Day two proved to be much tougher than the first. We hiked for seven hours, all of which were fairly demanding and technical. Tom did great! In fact, others complimented us on just how strongly the three of us worked as a team. (Again, a team consists of a blind climber and two sighted guides, one in front to provide directional commands and one in back to make sure the commands are met.)

We had another spectacular lunch along a ridgeline, giving us a much appreciated mid-day break. It was a large, flat, open area surrounded by rocks with wild flowers budding between the cracks. The views of the canyon below were spectacular. I have always been told to count my blessings, and by describing the views to Tom, I fully realized the significance of that advice.

*Tom celebrating that we made it to lunch*

Day two's climb peaked at 12,500 feet before we dropped back down to our campsite for the night at 12,335 feet. Camp that night was flatter and thankfully drier, but unfortunately not flat enough to avoid the "slip-n-slide;" however, our tents were more spread out, so I was hopeful we would have a quieter night. The drier ground did not equate to warmer temperatures though. I knew the importance of positive thoughts, yet I could not help but count down in my head our journey. We still had five more nights on the mountain, each one colder than the one before.

Dinner was served early and consisted of hot leek soup, chicken, rice, vegetables, and salad. While it may sound like an ample meal, for me it was not. I was a vegetable and chicken eater, salads being my "go to" meal. But this fare was not what I was used to. Tanzanian chicken is unlike anything I had seen before and, to be honest, quite unappealing. In fact, it was so unappealing that I never ate it. The soup was... well, liquid and warm with a hint of flavoring, but no visible ingredients (for the warmth alone, soup became something I looked forward to each night). The vegetables were flavorless and typically overcooked, and the salad consisted of a few pieces of lettuce per person—definitely not my usual, generous portion. The rice was the same simple white rice we get in the States. But in all fairness, considering that all our food and the kitchen setup each night to prepare it was carried on the backs of Sherpas, the menu was probably, by Tanzanian standards, *campsite gourmet.*

So far the views of the summit from both nights' campsites had more than made up for the food. Kevin commented that we were lucky the skies were so clear, making such unobstructed views possible. In fact, looking up into the darkness I was reminded of my grade-school field trips to the planetarium to learn about the constellations. Only here, on the side of the mountain, unlike the planetarium dome, the darkness provided the perfect black backdrop and the clarity magnified the brightness of the stars. In fact, the stars were far brighter than any I had ever seen. As I brushed my teeth before bed, I had an incredible view of the Milky Way. My field trips were being brought to life as I gazed up, stunned by the sheer magnitude of the night sky.

Showing concern for how cold I already was, Kevin let me in on a little secret. After dinner he filled my 1-liter neoprene bottle with left over hot tea and instructed me to cradle it between my knees in my sleeping bag. I did what he said and it was as though someone put a radiator in my bag. It worked like a gem.

## DAY THREE

The next morning was a bright and beautiful day as we set off for Lava Tower, the rock formation that marked our camp destination on day three. This day was promised to be an easier hike, but that promise only held true for the blind climbers who were willing to hold on to their guides' backpacks. For Tom and our team it proved to be another demanding challenge, this one nearly six and a half hours.

The terrain we had to traverse was a huge field strewn with large and medium-sized boulders. Tom was determined to maneuver through the boulders on his own, not holding on to the lead guide's backpack. Tom had never trained holding on to either of our packs and to suggest he do that now meant to him he would fall short of his intentions, his commitment to climb the mountain on his own. He chose to maneuver his way over the rough terrain by using only the sound of our voices and the two cowbells tied to the lead guide's trekking pole and backpack, helping to give him guidance and spatial awareness. This was no different than any of our training hikes or our days on the mountain together as a team so far. It just made for extremely slow progress, having us fall back from the rest of the group, but it didn't bother me. I was proud of his determination and focus and that he chose not to deviate from what he set out to do just because the hike on this day got tough.

Nonetheless, it was a taxing ordeal. With each stumble, Tom's frustration grew more and more apparent. Knowing that his actions were a direct result of my instructions, naturally my frustration began to grow as well. Later, back at the campsite, Tom would describe our hike that day as a kind of mental warfare he'd fought to keep himself focused on the information he had to sort through at every step.

Tom's description that night took me back to the very first training day we'd had together nearly a year ago. We had hiked a fairly flat section of a trail in Arizona known as Trail 100. As a guide I was encouraged to close my eyes to get a sense of what it felt like to hike blind. With each stub of my toe or the slightest stumble, I wanted to open my eyes to regain balance—and did a few times, not being able to control my reflex. Only I realized Tom didn't have that option—he could never "open" his eyes. He had to continue pushing forward even when he felt off balance.

As our training days continued, Kevin's concern for our slow pace grew. Kevin knew we had to pick up the training pace if we wanted to make camp in daylight each day on Kilimanjaro. Regardless of Tom's lack of sight and balance, he was expected to move just as fast as the rest of us. This is when I discovered the importance of giving detailed and accurate instructions. This is also when we discovered the additional sense of direction and value the cowbell provided.

Presently, traversing through the Kilimanjaro boulder fields, my instructions sounded something like this: *Turn 90 degrees to the right and take three steps. Turn left 45 degrees for five steps. Left foot up and over to the right 6 inches.* Imagine the concentration Tom had to maintain to move through a dark space with that much instruction for six solid hours.

Over time our team had fallen so far behind the others in the boulder-strewn field that they were no longer even within our sight. As we struggled on I felt like we were in one of those movies where someone is trekking across the desert—the scene where the vast breadth of the desert lands are scanned with only a tiny dot representing a person. We were that dot. I had never been so thankful in my life as I was for the one kind Sherpa who stayed with us, regardless of our pace, to show us the way.

*Team Hicks at the end of the boulder fields*

We reached 15,400 feet and made the final turn to descend down to our campsite at 14,680. Our team arrived just as everyone was about to enjoy a late lunch. We were so hungry, we threw our bags in our tents in record time to make it to lunch while there was still food left on the table. After eating we still had a few hours of daylight to do a little exploring. Our site was a large, open space with an incredible view of Lava Tower, a beautiful large rock formation perfectly positioned in the foreground of the summit. The visibility of the glaciers surrounding the summit was sharp, giving the impression that the distance was short and the highest peak could be reached in a few hours. So deceiving.

That night, sleeping at nearly 15,000 feet, meant bathroom urges came more frequently. Despite my efforts, it was impossible to make it through the night without going. It took me nearly an hour to face the inevitable and build up the courage to brave the cold. It is not as though I could head out to the bathroom half asleep, either. It required being completely awake and fully present for the entire process.

I had learned to store my headlamp in the side pocket of the tent for easy finding. I had also figured out the importance of placing any clothing I thought I might need, such as my heavy down coat, at the top of my compression bags. It is not much fun to dig through tiny bags with cold fingers in the middle of the night. However, I learned the hard way not to leave any article of clothing out of the bag entirely. Exposure to the cold air meant there would be a thin layer of frost covering it within hours, even inside the tent. And finally, once the layers were on, I'd slide to the end of the tent where my hiking boots were kept and get my feet into the cold, hard, and dirty boots. With gloves back on, hat secured over my ears, and a wad of toilet paper stuffed into my pocket, I was finally ready.

The minute I unzipped the tent and stuck my head out, the coldness took my breath away. My instinct was to retreat back into the tent, but now the bodily functions were engaged and there was no turning back. I managed to stand straight and looked out of the tent. The extra effort and struggle became totally worth it. I can still picture the clear black sky and brilliance of the stars that lighted its vast expanse. A smile reached from ear to ear on my face. I'm not even sure how long I stood there in total awe, but the biting cold was no longer the focus of my attention.

## DAY FOUR

The wake-up call on day four marked the coldest day so far, measuring only 21 degrees. It took pure will just to sit on top of my sleeping bag and get dressed for the day. The last thing I wanted to do was undress and expose even an inch of my skin, even if it was only for a brief moment. My tent mate and I both decided it was time to break out the long johns.

Breakfast was warm wheat porridge, toast with peanut butter, a tiny little egg, and a piece of sausage. Like the chicken from our supper, the sausage did not seem all that appealing. But turning down my sausage quickly brought about a kick to the shin under the table. My fellow climbers were reminding me to never turn down food. There would always be someone at the table to eat it.

I do not know if it was my love for peanut butter or if Tanzanian peanut butter really is the best in the world but, whatever the case, it became my favorite food. Every morning that followed, I would scan the breakfast table for the peanut butter jar. This became my main protein source. If left alone, I am certain I would have devoured the entire jar.

This day's hike actually descended about 2,000 feet. Not necessarily a tough hike, yet it proved to be a technical challenge for Tom with a lot of loose boulders on a steep downhill slope causing some slippage. We reached our next camp after a short three and a half hours—perfect time for a lunch of buttered toast, chicken, soup, and French fries. Only for me to eat fried food and buttery bread would invite a tummy ache, the last thing I wanted on the side of a mountain with no bathroom. By deduction, my lunch consisted of soup.

After lunch, we hiked a few miles to Paradise Falls, an amazing waterfall surrounded by a tropical setting and offset by a view of the snowcapped summit in the background. Truly an amazing sight like no other. It was a green oasis set in the middle of a landscape consisting of dirt and rock with a snowy, white border.

Getting to the falls required bush whacking through dense foliage and crossing a few fresh water streams. Attempting to take the perfect picture of the falls, Grahame slipped on a rock and rolled horizontally, luckily face up, in the stream. Thankfully he was unscathed, and we all enjoyed a good laugh at his expense. We then got concerned about drying his clothes for the next day's hike. Temperatures were still dropping, but luckily the clothes dried while spread out on top of a tent. Limited by the amount of clothes we could each bring, no one had extras.

That night's dinner was one of my favorites: zucchini soup for starters, then pasta with either beef or veggie broth. I chose the veggie. Perhaps what made it my favorite was the jar of peanut butter that made an evening appearance. I was able to recover the perfect amount from the bottom of the jar for my slice of toast. This made my night. Once the food was gone, the silence in the dinner tent was replaced with laughter from the onslaught of joke-telling and movie quotes.

The night grew late and we all decided we better retreat back to our tents. As I lay in my sleeping bag, hopeful that I would fall quickly asleep, my mind began to wander to the days still ahead. As much as I told myself to take one day at a time, looking up at the summit was quite intimidating. It was not so much the hiking challenge that concerned me as it was the increasing cold. We still had four more days, and I could not ignore that each one of them would be colder than the last.

I was also concerned about the unknown effects of the increasing altitude. Each night I had listened to the sounds of at least one person getting sick outside their tent. My heart would sink, and I would say a little prayer that it would pass so they would have the strength to continue on by morning. Some mornings I could hear the discussions between Kevin, Marc, and the doctor, one of the sighted guides, as to whether or not that person should continue. While they always tried to keep things quiet so as not to worry anyone, the campsites were small, so we all knew.

Would it be my turn next? Or would I be one of the lucky ones never affected? All I knew was I did not want to be the one they forced back down the mountain because of altitude sickness. I could not let Tom, the group, or myself down. But with all of that said, I forced myself to turn my thoughts toward the next day, which would be our climb up Barranco Wall.

## DAY FIVE

The day brought with it an unusually warm morning, considering we were at 13,000 feet. We set out for our hike just before 9:00 a.m., slightly later than our usual 8:00 or 8:30 start. Our route started out in the same direction as the previous day's excursion to Paradise Falls, taking us first over a few streams that had been partially frozen. Getting Tom across while keeping him dry became our first challenge of the day. With plenty of broad, dry rocks spanning the width of the stream to stand on, we had a variety of options.

Within a few hours the trail ended at the base of a massive rock wall known as the Barranco Wall. To reach the mesa that spanned across the top of the wall, we were required to climb with both hands holding vertically onto the sheer rock face as we shimmied up and around the wall with only the width of a narrow goat trail beneath our feet. One step in the wrong direction could lead to a fall and certain death below.

Now just imagine carrying this off blindfolded. For Tom, that's what it was like, but he surprised us all. In fact, he definitely moved faster up the wall than he did days before when traversing the boulder fields. It was as if the use of his hands gave him another sensory tool and thus a new source of confidence. Looking back, I was in awe of how far he had come since our first training workouts.

Just about a month prior, we were with the whole group on a hike up Humphreys Peak in Flagstaff, Arizona. Standing at 12,637 feet, Humphreys Peak is the highest of a group of extinct volcanic peaks known as the San Francisco Peaks. Our day on the mountain proved to be a wake-up call for many of us. Not only was Humphreys representative of the physically demanding terrain of Kilimanjaro, it was a good test of a hiker's ability to quickly adapt to a rapidly changing climate. The base of Humphreys was warm and sunny, but as the elevation increased, it was not uncommon for climate conditions to fluctuate drastically. The top portion of the mountain was typically covered in snow, which meant that the upper trails were a mixture of slippery mud, slush, or deep snow.

*Team Hicks training on Mt. Humphreys*

The worst scare I ever had guiding Tom was when we were coming down from the saddle of Humphreys. We hit a section of narrow trail covered in deep snow. The top layer glistened with ice, evidence it had begun to melt in the day but was now freezing over as the sun went down. With Tom's 6'4" frame came size 13 shoes, and let's just say he was not necessarily light on his feet. I can still see that one nearly fatal step. His foot landed close to the edge of the bank and slid on the frozen surface of the snow, causing him to lose his balance and literally roll down the side of the mountain, "ass over tea kettle," as the saying goes. I'm certain his bruised ribs reminded him of the fall for days, yet we were grateful for the tree that stopped his momentum. Unhurt and a little shaken up, Tom held on as Grahame and I hoisted him up and got him back on the trail.

Now here on Barranco Wall, one of the two days of our ascent that intimidated us the most (the second being the actual ascent to the summit), Tom moved gracefully and confidently up, over and around this massive rock formation. I think there were times my heart beat faster than his, but perhaps not having sight on this section of our trek actually worked in his favor. He had no idea at all of the consequences he'd suffer from making just one small move in the wrong direction.

It was another long, six-hour day, yet for Tom the adventure seemed to have given him a six-hour energy boost. As we rolled into our campsite, Tom was grinning ear to ear, relieved to have the Barranco Wall behind him. Back down at nearly 15,000 feet, the view was spectacular. I spent the next few minutes trying my best to describe to Tom the sensation I felt looking down on the tops of the clouds. It is one thing to see them from an airplane window, but completely different when the view is unobstructed and the panorama is spread out across the horizon.

The next few hours were typical of every night we'd already spent on the mountain: unpack, settle in, and clean up for dinner. Cleaning up consisted of a baby wipe bath and a change of clothes. Unfortunately, there were never any fresh, clean clothes.

The dinner tent was filled with the usual chatter of the climbers coming off of the day's hike. Only for me, I was not partaking. Something did not feel quite right. Not wanting to admit that I might be feeling the effects of the altitude, I did my best to keep a smile through dinner and hoped that no one noticed I did not eat. My tactic of moving my food around on my plate worked well.

Making my way back to my tent as soon as the opportunity presented itself, I changed into my nightly turtleneck and fleece jacket layers. For some reason the same layers that provided warmth in the past brought about a bad case of claustrophobia which then led to a nauseous feeling. I tugged at my neckline and unzipped my sleeping bag below my chest. In need of a distraction, I listened to my iPod the entire night. There was no way I wanted to be the one heaving outside my tent tonight. I would not allow my mind to think I could fall victim to altitude sickness.

## DAY SIX

I must have dozed off to sleep at some point with the music from my iPod still playing in my ears. The next sound I heard was that of the wake-up call. It was 6:30 a.m., and I still had an hour until breakfast. I went about my morning just as I had in the past, not allowing myself to give a thought to how I felt, and barely eating. It was not until I snapped on my backpack to head out that the nauseous and claustrophobic feeling returned. For some reason the fastener across my chest felt as though it was under my throat.

Less than 10 minutes into our hike, I was hunched over my trekking pole unable to move. That was all it took. Grahame took one look at me and asked the doctor for a Diamox pill, the medicine so many in the group had already been taking for their symptoms of altitude sickness. Why I was so stubborn the night before I will never know. Instantly I felt relief, and within 30 minutes I was my normal self again.

That day's hike was not one that offered us much pretty scenery, but it was our last one before camping for an early morning ascent to the summit next day. We hiked up a large slope to a ridgeline and then down the other side, through a valley, and up another steep climb. We hiked through a campsite known as Barafu Camp, where most climbers stop to stay the night before their summit. There were other climbers' tents set up but no one in sight. It was awful—loose slate everywhere with just enough space cleared between each tent. This desolate-looking campsite seemed like it was straight out of an old black-and-white science-fiction movie, and I was glad to move on.

Luckily, we had received special permission from the authorities for our group to hike another 60 minutes to the Kosovo Camp which sat just above 16,000 feet. This was truly a blessing. Not only was Kosovo an hour closer to the summit, it was much flatter and far more visually appealing.

Once situated, we ate an early dinner and were then ushered straight to bed, settling into our tents by 7:00 p.m. Tomorrow was the big day, Summit Day. Our wake up call would be 1:00 a.m. We had to be dressed, finished with breakfast, and in line, ready to move out by 2:00 a.m. At dinner Kevin had stressed the importance of an on-time departure. There would be absolutely no exceptions tomorrow. It is not uncommon for there to be dramatic changes in weather conditions with little or no notice on the way to the summit. To ensure a successful summit we needed to get to the top and head back down far enough before any storms rolled in.

With his other expeditions Kevin made the wake-up call at midnight for a 1:00 a.m. departure. However, with our group he was concerned about a few of us surviving the extremely cold weather. We had a couple of young boys, 12-13 years old, and a few with extremely low body fat, me included. He wanted to limit the time we were hiking in the darkest, coldest hours, yet still get us to the top before a potential storm hit. The window of time he was dealing with was very narrow.

Camp was so cold that night, I think I may have worn every article of clothing to bed that I'd brought. On the upside, I told myself, sleeping in all my clothes would make getting dressed in the morning that much easier. I actually slept fairly well that night, considering what lay ahead.

## DAY SEVEN: JUNE 29, 2009 — SUMMIT DAY

The 1:00 a.m. hour arrived and temperatures measured below freezing at 18 degrees. Managing to fit on a few more layers, I must have looked like the Michelin Man. Breakfast was only porridge and popcorn. Still a tad nauseous, I only ate a few handfuls of popcorn.

Bundled tightly with headlamp fastened, I joined my team to set out single file at 2:15 a.m. Temperatures continued to drop as we climbed. The last temperature I recall hearing was 11 degrees. I could not feel my feet, but somehow they carried me steadily up the ascending slope. We were instructed to take pressure breaths with each step, consisting of a regular inhalation with a deep exhalation. Climbing was slow and steady, yet many in the group were still out of breath and struggling. But not Tom. He kept a good pace and if he was miserable, he kept it to himself. Breathing was so precious, no one could speak, so complaints weren't an option.

*Tom in the breakfast tent summit morning*

I remember looking up occasionally toward what I assumed to be the summit, only to see distant rows of lights. Or were they stars? Surrounded by complete, almost eerie darkness, it was tough to distinguish between the stars and the lights from the headlamps of climbers who had gotten earlier starts. In fact the stars were so bright that one of the blind climbers later told the story of seeing stars for the first time. He was born blind and had never seen any kind of light, yet he described the light he saw from a star early that morning.

The sky was slowly beginning to glow, and by 7:00 a.m., when it was fully light, we reached our first rest area, Stella Point. From there, we set out on a wide, gradually winding path with views of vast glaciers spanning across a large crevasse between the mountain peaks. It was only one hour later that our three-person team, Team Hicks, was the first in the group to arrive and triumphantly approach the Uhuru Peak sign, a marker that indicated we had reached the summit.

*Tom and me at Stella Point*

I want to say that reading aloud the words that are carved into uneven wooden slates making up the sign: YOU ARE NOW AT THE UHURU PEAK, THE HIGHEST POINT IN AFRICA. ALTITUDE 5,859 METERS, was the most amazing moment in my life, but it wasn't. Much more amazing was the moment my blind teammate, Tom Hicks, brushed his fingers against the sign as I read it. Tears were running down his cheeks, expressing his deep gratitude for the guidance that had made this moment possible. He turned away from the sign, raised his hands above his head, and let out a cry of sheer joy.

*Tom and me reaching the Summit:*
*the single most impactful moment of my life*

Tom's face told the full story of the many trials and tribulations we'd shared in the past year of training together that had gotten us to this very place. Seeing the summit through my own eyes was spectacular, but seeing it through Tom Hick's "eyes" was something I believe will be seared in my memory forever.

We stayed at the summit for about 90 minutes, waiting for the other teams in our group and taking our share of pictures. While supplemental oxygen is not required at 19,340 feet, the air is thin enough that any extended stay could trigger headaches and other altitude-sickness symptoms. We took one last look, snapped a final photo, and began our descent.

*The team at the Summit*

The hike back down was much tougher than I expected. The early-morning hours had been so dark that I had not noticed the loose texture of the terrain on the way up, commonly referred to as *scree*. Scree is basically very fine, powder-like dirt. The quickest way down under such conditions is to ski, traversing the path from side to side as though on a pair of snow skis. Just like skiing through thin powder snow, a trail of fine particulate is kicked up behind, making visibility tough for anyone who follows close behind another. We had been forewarned to wear our glacier glasses and pack a handkerchief to wear as a mask for minimizing the amount of dirt inhaled. But it was rough going and at some point Tom became so fatigued it was difficult for us to guide him down. Luckily, two Sherpas were nearby and ended up bringing him back down to camp, each one taking one side to support him in his descent.

I am not sure how long it took to get back to Kosovo. I just recall seeing our campsite below and having the feeling, *We're almost there.* Yet as time passed and we continued downhill, the camp never seemed to get any closer. My legs grew more fatigued, and with the loss of altitude, my stomach was signaling a regained appetite.

At last, we took our final steps into camp. Before any of us were allowed in the lunch tent, we had to clean up. We were covered head to toe in fine scree, giving our faces the appearance of being made up with a dark brown bronzer. Time to put the baby wipes to the test. It was a good thing I packed more than one box.

We had 90 minutes to clean up, pack our belongings, and eat lunch. No rest for the weary! Kevin wanted us back out on the trail so we would reach our next campsite before dark, and we still had a long hike ahead of us.

I am not sure if it was fatigue or the unevenness of the ground on the descent that caused our three-person team to slow in pace, but we soon fell seriously behind the rest of our group. It took us another four and a half hours of non-stop hiking to reach Camp Millennium at 12,620 feet. Our biggest motivator to press on was the beer we'd been promised awaiting us at camp. We were told that the additional Sherpas would hike up from the Gate with bottles of ice-cold Kilimanjaro beer, which they would sell for just one dollar apiece. Even those who were not beer drinkers suddenly formed a craving and were motivated to keep pushing on to finally slake their thirst with this exotic treat.

Once again, Team Hicks was the last team into camp. Sure enough, about half our group was sitting around in a circle, enjoying their bottles of Kilimanjaro beer. We did not even attempt to find our tents before we cracked open our own bottles. Ah...it went down so smoothly—I can still recall the taste of it today. No doubt, it was the best beer around. Or perhaps my opinion was influenced by the last seven days of a rather restricted diet. Speaking of diet, either my clothes were stretching out with wear, or I had lost some serious weight.

Instead of celebrating late into the night, we ate dinner quickly and all went back in our tents to recover from the pure exhaustion of the day. Once again, the night brought cold temperatures, but now I didn't care. Tomorrow we would hike our final leg back down to the base of the mountain, load onto a bus, and head back to our resort for a hot shower, a real meal, and an actual bed. No more sounds of tent zippers!

## DAY EIGHT: FINAL DESCENT

I woke up the next day with an extra bounce in my step. Not remotely feeling like hiking, I was energized more by the comforts that awaited me at the bottom of the mountain. Getting dressed was actually comical. After seven days of rotating between the same two pairs of pants, three shirts, and three pairs of socks, I put the smell test to work.

"Ugh, not that pair of socks. They stink!" I muttered out loud as I rifled through my clothing pack. "Oh my, definitely not this pair either—they reek!" The third pair was my heavy summit day socks, far too thick for today's warmer hike. I settled for a stinky pair.

After breakfast, we gathered around for a final group photo and set out toward the gate at 8:45 a.m. Kevin estimated our hike to be five hours. But Tom was very exhausted, and hiking downhill proved to be tougher on him than going up. Thinking about it, it makes perfect sense. If I close my eyes, moving uphill I can use my foot to feel the ground before transferring my weight. Moving downhill, I really have no idea when to shift my weight. Needless to say, it took our team six and a half hours to reach the gate, making us the last team off the mountain.

I wish Tom could have seen the beauty of the rain forest we hiked through. The weather cooperated perfectly, fluctuating between a light drizzle and rain. Because it was a rain forest, and it was our last day, no one really seemed to care. In fact, I found it to be a fitting and memorable finale.

Our team really pulled together this day, our last day on the mountain. It was not easy traveling slowly. We just wanted to be done; we all wanted a hot shower and clean clothes. Packs became heavy, causing our lower backs to hurt. There was just enough rain to make the tree roots and rocks extremely slippery, adding to Tom's difficulty in hiking downhill. Fortunately, Kevin hung back with us and together we brought up the rear.

Once down the mountain, there was still another 30-45 minutes of flat hiking along a dirt road to get to the bus-loading zone. Now within cell phone reach, Kevin called Godlisten and Nixon, the owners of the expedition company in Africa he'd worked with to provide the Sherpas. Godlisten and Nixon drove a truck down the dirt road back up toward us. The four of us happily climbed into the back, standing up while holding on to roll bars as they drove us towards the gates.

I was not prepared for what awaited us. As the truck pulled in, we were literally surrounded by at least a hundred Sherpas greeting us with African songs, accompanied by clapping and dancing to the sound of guitars. Lifting us off the truck, they congratulated us one-by-one as though we were celebrities.

Around the corner a feast awaited. Tables of food piled high bordered the perimeter of a small grassy area. Sherpas lined up to wash our boots and clean off the outside of our daypacks, while small children waited anxiously by to show off their braided bracelets and hand-painted artwork for sale.

Here we had completed an eight-day journey, a journey so many had celebrated in the past, yet the Tanzanians treated us as though we were the first to have ever conquered Kilimanjaro. They treated us like royalty—like Olympians just having won a gold medal. The skin that covered my body that had just slumped the last six plus hours down the mountain was now covered with goose bumps. My walk was a little taller and my step regained its pep. The party had given us all a second wave of energy, energy I could feel radiating off each one of us.

It was that energy that carried us through a horrendously long bus ride. These buses were so old; I am surprised they could travel the rough roads of the country. Covered in eight days worth of dirt, we were packed in like a can of sardines, sitting five people across and knees tucked nearly to our chins. We joked how badly we must all have smelled, yet not a single nose could prove it. That is what happens when you smell equally as bad as your neighbor. From that moment on, we solidified the unique bond we would each carry for life.

My head did not hit the pillow that night until 11:00 p.m. I was running on a complete adrenaline high. While I expected to sleep like a log, I slept as though I was still on the mountain, listening to my iPod all night in an attempt to keep my mind from retracing everywhere I had just been.

## MAKING A DIFFERENCE

My eight days on Kilimanjaro were incredibly powerful. They made me realize just how impactful my actions over the previous year had been in preparation for this trip. Those days had meaning; they were purposeful. And that gave me a purpose and confirmation that my actions made a difference.

In addition, my commitment to this climb made a difference in Tom's life, his wife and children's lives, and every person he would later touch. I helped to make a difference in the lives of 350 infants at the Foundation who would now have early intervention care because of the money we raised. My efforts helped to make a difference to the countless visually impaired people who heard of our story and as a result have higher aspirations. I helped to make a difference in front of more than 7 million viewers who watched our story on the NBC broadcast and more than 3 million who watched on msnbc.com. I helped to make a difference for those people who now think differently when interacting with a visually impaired person because they heard our story on a local broadcast or read it in the countless newspapers that followed us. Perhaps they donate money, perhaps they employ someone with vision loss, or perhaps they volunteer their time—either way, there is a ripple effect far wider than I could have imagined.

That is just the ripple I created, but take that and multiply it by the other 24 people who climbed with me. Now that's impactful! Marc Ashton, the director of the organization that made it all possible, said it best: "Climbing a mountain is a great moment. Learning to read Braille is a lifetime success!"

Kevin, our expedition guide, told me from the beginning that the mountain was magical. Little did I realize just how magical it would turn out to be. He was not surprised when I shared with him my struggles, once home, to adapt back into my corporate lifestyle. He said most people find it difficult to conform back into the expectations of the workplace from their experience of freedom and adventure on the mountain.

I am not sure if my transition was any different than that of the others. All I can say is that I struggled. From that moment on, I wanted to know that everything I did, all the time, made a difference. I began evaluating every task I took on, looking for its importance, its purpose. What kind of an impact did I make in a day, a week, a month? Was I changing lives? Or was I caught in what many refer to as the rat race of life?

Over the years since Kili, this desire to make a difference has not seemed to lessen. I still ask myself the same questions. When I did not feel I was making a difference in the office, I would volunteer, or I would simply make an effort to do something nice for another. Every time I did, I not only knew I was helping others, but my eyes were opened to see the changes within myself. We all benefit from *giver's gain*.

Wikipedia defines giver's gain as "the belief that when people set goals to help others and honestly work to achieve these goals, they usually gain the most out of the experience – through a reciprocal benefit."

I learned on the mountain that when I tie my goal to helping others, I gain far more than the goal I set out to achieve. By simply doing what I love and giving more than I expect in return, I flourish the most. The mountain showed me that while I always thought I wanted "more," what I truly wanted was for my life to stand for "more."

## Play #2:  Connect to Your Passion

We are all naturally driven by a purpose. Some people have greater clarity in defining their passion—what motivates and inspires them—and thus live a purpose-driven life. For others, passions may be cloudy, muddling their life purpose. Regardless, everyone wants to be connected to others. It is human nature to desire affiliation with a cause greater than oneself.

Living with an intention, connected to a cause, requires full engagement. When you live with intention, everything you do is purpose-driven, and under your purpose lies your passion. When you become intentional in your actions, your life is filled with joy. Your life is fuller and, in return, more fulfilling.

In this chapter, we explored the notion of Giver's Gain, the idea that when people set goals to help others, they often receive tremendous value back. A great way to find your passion, the things that truly add value to your life, is to look at times when you have helped to make a difference in the lives of others, and it felt priceless.

## Kristy's Game Time Coaching
## Journal Entry

When in life have you been driven by something bigger than yourself? Were you involved in volunteer work or a particular organization that motivated you to become a better person than who you saw yourself as? Or were you working with a person who inspired you to raise the bar beyond your norm? Describe the event in detail. What was the experience like? What were you doing? How did you feel?

After completing your journal entry, circle all the words describing your emotions behind the activity. When living with intention, it is these emotions you want to recreate, not necessarily the event itself.

# CHAPTER 3

# THE POWER OF BEING PRESENT: ALCATRAZ CHALLENGE

*It's all about the journey, not the outcome.*
—Carl Lewis

After Kilimanjaro, life returned to normal. Or did it? For me, Kilimanjaro created a new kind of normal. I became far more critical of how I spent my time, thinking twice about my intentions behind each activity. My sense that life had more to offer was now translated into the strong belief that my life *should* and *could* stand for more. I knew that riding the high and basking in a sense of fulfillment from climbing the mountain with Tom had a shelf life, and soon I would need another challenge. Simply put, I felt lost without a focus that continually challenged me.

Prior to my back fracture, I ran marathons. Since running became my hobby in 2000, it never occurred to me to choose anything but running as my next goal. It was more a question of what race I wanted to train for next. At this point, I had completed nine marathons, including Boston, so the easy answer would be for me to run a 10th - a nice round number. Yet I lacked the desire to once again train the distance needed for me to be competitive. I wanted to do something new and different.

## A SEED IS PLANTED

One morning at my Masters Swim class, I found myself in a conversation with a doctor who had been swimming in the lane next to me. He began telling me about the time he had swum Alcatraz, the now defunct but famous federal penitentiary in the middle of San Francisco Bay. Within the hour I left the pool and declared that my next adventure would be conquering the bone-chilling, shark-infested, strong current waters of the San Francisco Bay. That day I researched organized races and found The Alcatraz Challenge, a race that consisted of a swim from Alcatraz to shore, followed by a 7-mile run across the Golden Gate Bridge. If I wanted to do that one, I had less than 11 months to learn how to swim more than 50 meters at a time and without the use of a pull buoy.

The months that followed my decision were filled with countless drills and many agonizing days. I was often left feeling as though my lungs would never fill up with enough air to make it to the end of my lap lane. There was definitely something very different about breathing when I wanted to as I did in running versus breathing only during timed intervals as my face went in and out of the water. This observation made me think there had to be more to mastering this sport. Was there a mental element I had not yet identified?

*Training in the pool*

For some reason the mental block most commonly expressed by people who swam Alcatraz did not seem to faze me in the least. The San Francisco Bay is home to 11 different shark species, which did not concern me. However, that did not leave me any shortage of things to fear. My concerns were more mundane but just as terrifying to me as being eaten by a shark. Could I actually swim the 1.5 to 2 miles—distance varies depending on the course a swimmer takes—without resting? Could I withstand the elements, including water temperatures measuring in the low to mid 50s and currents that constantly changed direction? Could I stay within the course boundaries all the way across, not allowing the current to carry me too far off to be picked up by a kayak? I was told that if I did nothing, just lay in the water, the Bay currents would carry me out under the Golden Gate Bridge and off into the ocean in less than 30 minutes.

Then there were the stories from countless people who told me that the minute I hit the cold water, all of my blood would flow to my extremities and away from my heart, leaving me feeling breathless and anxious. Apparently, it is not uncommon for swimmers to have panic attacks. And the last time I checked, the Bay did not offer a pool edge to stop and hold onto while I caught my breath.

In addition to learning to swim nonstop more than just 50 meters at a time, hypothermia would be a major concern. While I would be wearing the thickest possible wetsuit allowed and drinking the recommended warm liquids prior to the race to increase my body temperature from the inside, I knew the best way to avoid hypothermia was to spend less time in the water. This meant I needed to learn to swim faster and get myself out of the water sooner.

Despite all of these concerns, I had the wherewithal to realize that completing this race, especially the part in the water, would more than anything be a mind game. As long as I built enough physical endurance to swim the distance, the rest of the challenge, consisting of my fears and concerns, could be overcome. Like training for running I would need to slowly increase my distance and time in the water and pair that training with some shorter, more intense swim sets to build endurance. I reminded myself that I did not start out running marathons the first day I laced up my running shoes. I knew well how to utilize *periodization* in my marathon training; the same concept would apply here.

Periodization involves the progressive cycling of different aspects of a training program during a specific period of time. The aim is to introduce new movements as you progress through the larger training cycle right up until the start of the event. For example, when running, I would cycle through workouts of speed and workouts of distance, slowly increasing each for two to three weeks. I would then insert a recovery week where my distance and intensity would decrease. The benefit of a recovery week is to allow my body to recover while still working out, referred to as an *active recovery*. My intensity and distance would increase again for the next cycle of 2 to 3 weeks following the recovery week, taking me beyond where I had been previously.

My confidence on the mental side, which I knew to be equally important, was not as strong. Sure, I had confidence in my ability to push through pain and discomfort. I trained and raced with the belief that pain is temporary, reward is permanent. However, when I ran, my feet were on the ground, I could see everything around me, and I could take a breath whenever I wanted to. If for some reason I had a cramp or got too tired to keep going, I could just stop. At least I had that option.

Swimming was different though. My feet would not be on the ground. In fact, the ground would be 100 feet below me. My sight would be limited. The water is so dark, I wouldn't see much of anything most of the time. And with the quickness of my breaths, would I even see the other swimmers? If I did get a cramp or fatigued, what would I do? There would be nothing around me to hold on to, and I doubted anyone would hear my cries for help.

While my mind would flood with these crazy thoughts from time to time, deep down I knew I had to find a state of inner peace. I had signed up for this race and I was determined to finish. Hundreds of people successfully swim the San Francisco Bay every year. I wanted to be one of them.

## POWER OF MIND

To give myself an edge in what I knew would be a major mental battle, I began reading about the power of the mind and getting inspired about all the things people can accomplish just by believing they can. I ran across what soon became some of my favorite quotes, which I posted around my house to give me constant positive reinforcement. Here are a few that worked especially well:

*What your mind can conceive and your heart believe, you can achieve.*
—Unknown

*Dream lofty dreams, and as you dream, so shall you become.*
—James Allen

*Our aspirations are our possibilities.*
—Robert Browning

*Limits begin where visions end.*
—Unknown

*The will of God will never take you where the grace of God will not protect you.*
—Unknown

Throughout the many months of training whenever I had fear or self-doubt, I would read these quotes. However, it was not until the race weekend and my flight out to San Francisco that I read the one piece of advice that stuck with me the entire race and served as my mainstay in actually being able to finish the race.

I had picked up a condensed copy of Eckhart Tolle's *The Power of Now,* and reading it on the plane, I found my secret weapon. In summary, he reminds us that as long as we are present and live in the moment, fear cannot exist. Fear only exists in the unknown, yet we are only capable of dealing with the here and now—what is present in this very moment. It is truly impossible to deal with something that has not yet even happened.

For me reading this was an "aha" moment. I was forced to re-examine my fears: So the breathlessness and anxiety people report as they hit the water and feel the shock of the coldness—that may or may not actually happen to me? The currents may or may not carry me under the Golden Gate Bridge and off into the ocean? I may or may not be struck down by hypothermia? It was in that moment I realized that allowing these thoughts, these questions of the unknown, to enter my mind was not productive. Furthermore, those were all other people's experiences. They were not my own, and they might never be.

What Tolle was talking about was not a new concept. I'd heard reference to the "power of now" before and the effectiveness of staying present. It makes logical sense for sure, but the bigger question I had was how to control my mind from going to all those fearful places. And wasn't it my responsibility to consider all of the possibilities? Certainly I would want to be prepared if anything like what I feared actually did happen.

The key for me in the passage I read was the simplicity of fear being absent, not even existing, when I simply choose to live in the moment. In the moment is where I can be fully responsible and deal with all the possibilities. I had never stopped to think that I am truly only capable of dealing with the here and now—the present moment. There is no possible way to take action on something that has not yet happened.

*WOW!* All these years I had been thinking I lived in the moment, yet if I truly did, I would have never experienced a state of fear. Even further, this meant that all of the energy I'd spent worrying about things in the past was wasted and could have been avoided by simply applying this one simple concept. From that moment forward, the idea of the power of now never left my thoughts.

The test of my new resolve came swiftly. Later that night, as the participants gathered for a briefing, I listened nervously to the race organizers telling us about which buildings along the shoreline to sight as landmarks to stay on course and the importance of raising our internal core temperature on the morning of the race before entering the water. Naturally, I began to feel anxious. It did not help matters when they announced that water temperatures were on the low end, and forecasts were predicting a rough chop—a far cry from ideal race conditions.

As the buzz in the room grew, I reminded myself of my secret weapon: be present in the here and now. I told myself: *At this very moment I am sitting in a warm room listening to instructions. That's all. That is all I am doing right now. There is nothing to be fearful of in this room where I am sitting.*

With each task in the preparation process, I continued to replay this message in my head. I found comfort in breaking every thought down into the reality of where my focus was at the time. As I drove along the foggy coastline towards my hotel, as I checked in and found my room, the message I gave myself was the same: *Stay focused on the task at hand.*

Once inside my room, my focus turned toward getting organized for the race. As I unpacked my bags and saw my gear, panic started to creep back in. In the blink of an eye, my mind began the familiar line of questioning: *Will the water be too cold for me to handle? Will the waves be too large and powerful for me to swim through? Will the current pull me off course?*

*Snap out of it*, I told myself. Regaining my composure, I brought myself back to reality. Right now, all thoughts need to be of the present, ensuring I had everything organized for my early morning wake-up call. *This is it.* In less than 12 hours, I will be in the water, fulfilling another bucket-list challenge of a lifetime.

The next thing I knew, it was time for lights out. My priority in that present moment was to get a full night of restful sleep. And I did.

## RACE DAY

It was the sound of my alarm clock that thankfully brought me to full attention the next morning. With no time built in my schedule to lie around in bed, I quickly got dressed. First my swimsuit and then a few layers of warm clothes. Next item on my agenda was a hot breakfast. I gathered up my precooked egg whites and container of oatmeal, premixed with cinnamon and Splenda, and headed downstairs to the hotel's breakfast area. Duly noting the advice given at the briefing the night before, I'd made arrangements with the hotel receptionist to have access to their microwave before they opened. No sense in ignoring the advice of eating a hot breakfast.

The only things left were to brush my teeth, gather up my transition bag, and head to the car. The transition bag was filled with my running clothes and shoes and would be placed according to my race number in an area at the finish of the swim.

Check-in was at the transition area, the East Beach of Crissy Field where I would exit the water and transition into the run start. The drive over went faster than I anticipated and parking was even easier. It appeared as though I'd beaten the rush of the other 599 participants who would soon descend upon the scene.

After finding my numbered transition spot, I set up my area to expedite a smooth change out of my wetsuit into my running clothes. It was finally time to shimmy into my wetsuit and find my way to the trolley, which would serve as the first mode of transportation to the race start. Things were definitely becoming more real by the minute. I found myself using my secret weapon constantly, reminding myself of exactly what I was doing in each moment in order to keep my thoughts in check. It may seem elementary, yet it was necessary and effective to settle my nerves.

The trolley ride took what felt like an eternity to go from the check-in area to the dock where we would board the barge to drive out to Alcatraz Island. I listened to people around me giving others advice. The buzz was centered on talk of the cold water and the strong currents that awaited us. Again, I found myself calming my anxiety by reminding myself to be in the very moment, not in fears. *You are sitting on the trolley, a tad cold— yet nonetheless, just sitting here*, I thought.

At the dock, we confronted the final drop bag bin. This is the last place participants can drop anything they don't want to carry with them in the race. This means shoes, gloves, and extra layers of clothing—all must be put in a bag marked with the person's race number and dropped into a bin. The next stop was the barge that would take us across the Bay to Alcatraz.

All 600 of us went across in the one barge. Standing shoulder to shoulder with my 599 competitors, I looked out the windows and listening carefully as the race organizers once again pointed out the buildings along the shoreline we were to keep in our sight during the swim so we'd be sure to stay on course. Finally *en route* to the famous Alcatraz Island, there was no turning back.

I don't recall exactly how long the barge took to arrive at Alcatraz. As my mind struggled to stay present, it seemed like an hour. On the other hand, as we approached and "The Rock" grew larger, the trip out didn't seem nearly long enough. There was no way for the barge to tie up to the island and the waters were far too deep to drop anchor quickly. It was clear the captain was working hard against the currents to hold the barge in one spot as we awaited the starting bell. The nervous energy that filled the cabin was palpable.

Tradition is to sing the national anthem before any sporting event. Since a professional was not hired, we all sang *a cappella* in unison and quite out of tune. I'm the type that gets chills every time the national anthem is sung, and this time not only did I have chills, but I could feel tears well up in the back of my eyes as we all put our voices together. Song over, I said a silent prayer and then it was "game on."

The time had come to layer on my double swim cap and lower my mask-sized goggles I'd bought to keep my face hopefully a little warmer than typical swim goggles. I wanted to be completely ready to make my jump into the water the second my turn came. Once the gun goes off, 600 swimmers must exit the barge through two double doors within a five-minute window in order to catch the current at the right time. Race officials stand at both doors, urging us on by yelling, "Right, center, left! Right, center, left!" signaling for the swimmers waiting in that position to take the plunge into the water. As soon as the swimmer hits the water, they must immediately begin swimming, first to get out of the way of the next person jumping in behind them and second to ensure the currents do not carry them too far off course. Yes, it actually happens that quickly!

As I was making my way to the double doors that were nearest to me, I was watching swimmers hit the water and begin swimming, taking note of what I was to do when it was my turn. I clearly remember one swimmer being picked up by a kayak within seconds of being in the water because he had already drifted too far west toward the bridge and would never be able to regain his course. Watching this entire process take place, I forced myself to repeat over and over in my mind, *You are standing in line on the barge, you are standing in line on the barge...*

The next thing I knew, my toes were on the line at the edge of the barge and I was looking down into the water. As soon as I heard the command, without thinking, I jumped into the water. We were all jumping in so fast that I hit the foot of the swimmer ahead in the water, but I remained unfazed. I put my head down and began swimming. In my mind, I repeated, *You are swimming. You are swimming.* And then it turned to, *WOW, you are really swimming. Oh my goodness. You are really doing this!* It must have been a good 10 or 15 minutes that passed before I realized I'd never felt the anxiety so many had described. I'd never felt that breathless feeling from the cold so many told me I would. A smile formed on my face under the water. *It worked! Being present really works.* I felt not one single ounce of fear.

Encouraged by this smooth beginning I continued to savor every single moment of the swim. The images are still so clear in my mind. I remember the powerful feeling of the currents, the change in the water from what seemed like 5 to 6 foot waves making it impossible to see anything unless from the top of a wave, to the short fast chop coming at me from the west. I focused on the bright red color of the Golden Gate Bridge every time my face turned to the right for a breath. I clearly remember the sea gulls soaring overhead and the occasional swimmer bumping up next to me. At one point I quickly flipped over onto my back so I could look back at Alcatraz. This was my one opportunity to see it from the water and I didn't want to miss that. How different it looked! The rock the prison sat on, viewed from the waters below it, loomed up above me. It had never looked so big!

Remembering the briefing from the night before, I ended my little break quickly. I needed to keep swimming so I could maintain my course and not get swept up by the current. Much to my surprise I found it easy to focus on the landmarks along the shore and knew just when to switch my focus from one to the next. I frequently checked the position of the kayaks that marked the east-west boundaries of my course and the larger boats that were strategically positioned just beyond. My goal was to estimate the middle and stay in it, allowing some leeway on either side as the race went on.

In the beginning other swimmers were bumping into me with some frequency, assuring me I wasn't out there alone. As the time grew, so did the distance between the other swimmers and me. I remember at one point, looking up to sight my next shoreline landmark, only to see a vast sea of choppy dark waves. Not a single kayak, boat or a single swimmer's cap in the water. For a split second I had a feeling that I was lost and completely alone. I hoped that some kayaker or boater had their eye one me. I did not want to end up a statistic, a 30-something woman swept under the Golden Gate Bridge and lost at sea, never to be found alive.

*But wait, that's not even rational!* I asked myself, *How could I possibly be alone when I was with 599 other swimmers and countless volunteers?* My heartbeat began to settle back down. I continued to swim, focusing on sighting the series of shoreline landmarks, reassuring myself that in time, I would see someone else. Sure enough, a few minutes later I saw a swim cap bobbling over the waves a few hundred meters away. After a few more breaths I could see the outline of a kayak to my right. *Whew, I was still on course*, I reassured myself.

It was not until an hour into the race, with the finish line in sight, that my hands, feet, and face began to feel numb from the cold water. It was then that the shore never seemed to get any closer. Or at least not fast enough in my mind.

*Keep swimming*, I told myself over and over.

I tried picking up the pace to increase the blood flow and get me out of the water that much sooner. Ever so slightly, the finish line banner grew just a little bigger and the spectators flanking each side grew more visible to my eye.

Finally, I reached the shoreline and pulled my feet up under my body so I could stand up. The wet sand felt like tiny needles piercing the bottoms of my bare feet. I had to consciously tell my feet to take steps forward. The swimmers who crawled out of the waters behind me were now running past me into the transition area. I was in a happy state of shock, so proud that I had made it to shore without falling off course and without being picked up by a kayak. I was grinning from ear to ear and thinking, *You did it! You actually swam Alcatraz!*

I was so stunned that I'd actually completed the swim, I completely forgot about the second half of the race, the 7-mile run across the Golden Gate Bridge.

## IT'S NOT OVER

Finally out of the water and working my way up the gradual incline of the beach, I heard someone call my name. It was one of the race officials who had given the briefing the night before. He apparently remembered me from my plethora of questions that followed the presentation. After congratulating me for making it through the swim, he quickly reminded me I still had more of the race ahead. Later, when I checked my results, I found that I had came out of the water with the first half of swimmers (the faster half)—not bad for someone who hadn't been racing for time, only wanting to finish.

Coming to my senses, I hurried over to my transition area and began the process of stripping off my wetsuit. As I struggled to get my second foot out, another swimmer offered to help by pulling my wetsuit until it came completely off with a final snap.

Putting on my running gear, especially my socks over my frozen feet, was a feeling I'd never fully anticipated. The numbness of my feet made it difficult to tell if my socks were on straight without any creases. Taking those first few steps were a tad painful, yet I didn't mind. All I could think was that I had survived the swim!

Still in the mindset of taking in every single moment of the experience, I decided I was going to smile and give words of encouragement to every runner I saw along the course. The course begins along the boardwalk which cuts through the middle of the sandy beach. About a mile down the boardwalk, the race path arrows point to a hard left toward a set of zigzagging stairs. At the top, I was directed by a race official to make a winding curve, followed by a 90-degree turn that would take me through a short tunnel with a caution sign, reminding the taller runners to duck when running through. Standing 5 foot, 2 inches, this didn't apply to me. The light at the end of the tunnel marked the point where we emptied directly out onto the Golden Gate Bridge. Finally, I reached the point on the run course I'd been waiting for.

Running across the bridge gave me a new perspective on the huge span of waters I'd just swum across: a sight of pure beauty. As I ran I found myself looking out over the Bay at the other swimmers still in the water, in awe that I'd swum that entire distance. Since the bridge was not closed to pedestrians I was forced out of my trance to avoid a near head-on collision with a tourist stopped to take pictures. It wasn't but a few steps later that I found myself staring back out over the water. I couldn't help it. I was overjoyed and exhilarated at what I'd accomplished.

The turnaround point was just beyond the other end of the bridge. In most out-and-back races, I'm thrilled to see the halfway sign, knowing that all I have to do is retrace my steps. But this time, I actually felt a little let down. It meant I was halfway to the end of my experience. With still more fuel in the tank, I put a little extra bounce into my step as I ran back across the bridge, passing other competitors, and cheering on those still heading out to the turnaround. Through the tunnel, sharp turn, around the curve, and down the stairs, I was quickly back on the boardwalk. I was amazed to see how many runners were still starting their 7-mile journey across the bridge.

Rounding the final turn, I got a full view of the finish-line banner. Crossing the line gave me the same feeling I'd felt when I crossed the finish line of my very first race, only 10 years earlier. I had survived and was relishing every moment.

Finishing this race was an event that marked another monumental point in my life. My results were impressive: I had finished 13th in my age division and 43rd overall for women in total swim and run time. This victory marked not only the physical accomplishment, but more importantly, the mental accomplishment of actively using my thoughts to overcome fear. From this moment forward, the phrase *Power of Now* would take on an entirely new meaning.

## MY EPIPHANY

What I took from Eckhart Tolle's book made an everlasting impact on my life. If I am present, living in the moment, fear cannot exist. Fear is only a projection of something I feel which may or may not happen. The key point to remember is it has not happened. And it may not ever happen.

I'm not saying that by living your life "in the moment" we never feel fearful. In fact, fear can be a natural and healthy emotion. Applying Tolle's philosophy, if I see another car swerve into my lane on the freeway, I can still be fearful it might hit me. While this is still a fear of something that has not yet happened, there was a specific action that caused the feeling of fear. My fear is a warning to me that I need to react by stepping on the brake or looking in the mirror to see if I can move into the next lane and be out of harm's way. Feeling fear is leading me to a positive reaction to avoid a collision. This is living in the moment. I'm reacting to something that is actually happening at that present moment.

But so many times fear can immobilize us. It stops us from going after the things in life we really want or from trying something new. Many times my fearful thoughts lead to the phrase, *I can't*, followed by all of the reasons why I can't. When I take the time to stop and think about my justifications of *I can't,* I realize they are all things that may or may not happen. They are simply a list of negative possibilities.

For every negative outcome, if I chose, I could find its opposite, a positive result. In most circumstances involving the unknown, positive results are just as likely to happen as negative results. Yet when I am projecting fear I am not thinking in terms of positive outcomes. When I let fear drive that list of possibilities, the list is full of self-defeating, self-limiting thoughts.

This reminds me of the expression, *We are our own worst enemy*. Or, *We are our own worst critic*. The vast majority of people live their life allowing fear to set limitations on what they can achieve. Yet if I apply this lesson, and fight fear with presence, those limitations would be lifted.

Once I bring myself back into the reality of the present moment, fear disappears. I calm down and am able to know what is simply factual. In that state of clarity I can make decisions that will have a higher probability of yielding the outcome I desire. I can turn my list of negative possibilities into a list of fulfilling, rewarding thoughts.

## THE NEXT CHALLENGE

It was not long before I was looking back on Alcatraz as just one more accomplishment to check off the list. Sure, I'm proud to say I swam Alcatraz. It was an amazing experience, a great story, and I learned a valuable lesson. The cold waters of the San Francisco Bay taught me something I would continue to practice—and test—in my future challenges—and one essential to becoming unstoppable.

The one thing my Alcatraz adventure did not do, however, was satisfy my thirst for conquering new challenges. The very next day at Masters swim class, my coach and one of the other swimmers suggested I do an Ironman. This is the ultimate triathlon, consisting of these three stages—swimming 2.4, biking 112, and running 26.2 miles. In isolation, any one of these stages would be a challenging endurance race. Ironman puts them all together in one race with no break.

The original idea of the Ironman began with a conversation between John Collins, a Naval Officer stationed in Hawaii, and his wife during a Waikiki Swim Club awards banquet the couple was attending. They began talking about the idea of combining the three toughest endurance races on the island into one. The challenge became reality on February 18, 1978 when 15 competitors, including Collins, came to the shores of Waikiki to accept the first-ever Ironman Challenge. Today, the recognition continues when athletes from around the world challenge themselves to prove the "Anything is Possible" mantra that was marketed by Ironman, the company, in 2012.

I had to laugh at my coach's suggestion that I do an Ironman. I did not even own a bike. In fact, I had only ridden a bike once or twice since my childhood years. No, Ironman was not it, not something I wanted to take on at the time. But little did I know that morning that the idea was planted like a seed, to stay with me in the back of my mind to eventually take root and blossom.

Looking back on the past year of my life, I had gone from having a fractured sacrum to leading a blind veteran to the summit of Mt. Kilimanjaro to swimming Alcatraz. I had successfully turned the adversity of my fracture into a new hope of swimming—a major accomplishment. But what had

I done with the life purpose I discovered on the mountain? I had made a vow to myself that everything I did moving forward would be for the betterment of someone else, a cause greater than my own ego. How quickly I'd lost sight of that resolve. I had three elements of the unstoppable equation now uncovered—meeting adversity with hope, finding my purpose in life, and using my mind to stay present and overcome fear. I had just not yet mastered the ability to put them all together.

But my next challenge would change that.

## *Play #3: Allow Presence of Mind to Be Your Guide*

By simply allowing yourself to slow down and be present you become fully engaged in the task at hand. While being fully engaged you have the opportunity to evaluate whatever is showing up. Are you focusing your time and energy on the things that are most important in your life? Are you driven toward the right goals?

Your actions will influence your beliefs and feelings, so you better be sure you are making good use of your time. Your beliefs and feelings will also drive your actions, increasing the importance of living a life of intention. Through repetition, your core beliefs will become conditioned to your new ways of thinking.

Habits are hard to break. Often this requires that you move from something that is very ritualistic and comfortable in your life to something unknown. The unknown can be a catalyst for fear. Realizing that F.E.A.R. is nothing more than False Expectation Altering Realty, will help you stay present. Fear is essentially a projection of what you think might or might not occur at some point in the future. By living in the present rather than living through projections of "what if" scenarios of the future, you are empowered to enjoy the moments that belong to your journey. When fear exists it becomes difficult to let go of a current situation, even when the situation is not serving you well and preventing you from moving toward what you want.

# Kristy's Game Time Coaching
## Journal Entry

Take a moment to slow down enough to be present. What is showing up? Are you focusing your time and energy on the things that are most important? Are you driven toward the right goals? What is motivating you?

Are there things standing in the way of what you want? If so, what is holding you back from moving toward your goals?

Once you are present, you can clearly identify the things that are most important, the things you aspire toward. Allow your presence to be your guide. Take a look at these things through different lenses, a new perspective. Are there changes you want to make?

Create positive triggers around these changes and place them where you can see them throughout the day. Triggers are visual reminders that generate constant reinforcement of your new way of thinking. An example is writing a few of your favorite inspiriting quotes on Post-Its and placing them on your mirror.

# CHAPTER 4

# ADAPTING TO CHANGE: THE ROPES

*Ten percent of life is what happens to us, and 90 percent is how we choose to react to it.*
—Unknown

The Alcatraz Challenge was behind me and I was open to the next adventure. This time, instead of a physical challenge, I was presented with an educational one. I was introduced to a series of leadership seminars that promised to uncover any subconscious blocks I might have that held me back from achieving success and freedom in all my life pursuits—to becoming unstoppable. Holding true to my motto, *Live with No Regrets*, I accepted the challenge. I was not so confident to think I didn't have my fair share of limitations and signed up with the intent to learn more about myself.

The series began with a weekend course in Arizona. While the sessions were packed full of opportunities to reflect on my beliefs and how those beliefs were providing results in my life, I did not jump at the opportunity to register for the next course in the series. It actually took talking to several people to convince me otherwise. I was assured that the second course was where the breakthroughs would occur. This first course was the prerequisite to get me there.

The second course was a seven-day retreat held on a beautiful remote property away from civilization for the entire week. I would be cut off from any form of outside communication or technology; allowed not even as much as an iPod to listen to music. The purpose was to provide an atmosphere of full engagement and connection, allowing the maximum opportunity for self-discovery. I quickly found myself in agreement—the more time I had for myself, I figured, the more I would be able to turn inward for guidance.

As skeptical as I was going in, I have to admit it was an amazing week. Classes were not given in a typical seminar setting, but rather consisted of many interactive processes and activities, involving others as partners and in small groups. In addition, there was even more time to experience things for myself. For example, there were physical activities that would allow me to draw my own conclusions about how I might or might not be creating desired outcomes in life. None of the facilitators were there to tell me what I should be doing or what would work for me. Their sole job was to provide an environment for self-discovery. It was up to me to pull it all together and draw my own conclusions.

## ROPE DAYS

While I discovered many things about myself during the seven days, there is one lesson in particular worth sharing.

We spent two full days outdoors with no classroom or seminar work. The first of the two days is referred to as "low-rope" day and the second as "high rope." Low rope day included activities that are just a few feet off the ground, so helmets and peer spotting were required. This day would help prepare us for high-rope day. On high-rope day an adventure company came onto the property to ensure our safety by appropriately securing harnesses and helmets for participants before each event.

Low-rope day was comprised of five activities, and consistent with most things in my life, I breezed through the first four challenges with complete success. It was not until the final activity, which involved walking across a tight wire that my luck seemed to change. The goal of this exercise was to walk across a wire suspended 3 feet above the ground. My partner would also walk across the same wire from the opposite end, the goal being to meet in the middle.

It was my turn. With our helmets on, my partner and I mounted the wire at opposite ends. *This should be a piece of cake,* I thought to myself. Yet for some reason as I moved across the wire toward the midpoint my legs began to shake. The more I told my legs to stop shaking, the worse they seemed to get. My mind began to race. *What was happening?*

With each step my legs seemed to tremble more. Thinking back a few months to what I learned about fear at Alcatraz, I had to wonder: *Was I afraid?*

*No,* I answered in my head.

*Then stop shaking,* I silently demanded.

I remember then saying to myself: *If your legs continue to shake, you will fall before you reach the middle.* I also questioned my own efforts: *How is it that the people who went before me, who are completely out of shape, made this look so easy?*

Nothing seemed to work. The wire began to shake so much I'm amazed I did not knock my partner off. After just a few more small steps it was over. I had fallen.

It wasn't physical pain I felt from the fall. My hurt pride was more intense than anything I felt in my body. I had broken my perfect streak for the day. I had failed. And failing this one exercise automatically made me feel as though I had failed the entire day.

It took a while, but eventually I came around to remembering what we'd been told in a preparation session. These low-rope exercises were not developed to test my physical ability. They were developed so I could see firsthand how *my state of being,* not my actions, impacted my results. Thoughts become actions, and actions become things. Did my thoughts create outcomes that I wanted? Or did they lead to outcomes I did not want? This was getting to the unconscious areas that would stop me from achieving my goal, and these exercises were designed to give me insight about how my thinking would determine the outcome.

At the end of each exercise, I was to evaluate my state of being throughout that particular exercise. In other words, what my mindset was rather than how I had actually performed. And the bigger question: Did that mindset produce the results I wanted? An example might be, was I fearful or was I courageous? And what was the result of being one way or the other?

I spent more time looking back at the thoughts running through my mind during this final tight-wire exercise than any other exercise that day. What was I thinking? What was I telling myself? How was I *being*?

In the past, such as when I'd overcome a broken back to climb Kili, I made the decision to change my attitude and found a way around what seemed like an insurmountable obstacle. When swimming Alcatraz, I had the power of staying in the present moment and moved myself away from fear. I thought I had the same level of commitment going into this exercise, telling myself, *This is easy. I can do this.*

But when things did not unfold exactly how I had envisioned, my thoughts turned negative, focusing more on what *not* to do instead of what to do. *Do not let your legs shake*, I'd told myself. Not only did I allow my thoughts to have a negative spin, I tied my execution to a negative outcome. *Because I am shaking, I will fall and not make it to the middle. Therefore, I will fail.*

I was completely focused on the end result—not on the journey. Not only was I not present, but I had mapped out my journey, exactly how I would execute it, and shaking wasn't part of my plan. I had envisioned my journey to be steady, walking with ease and balance. The minute my plan was disrupted, my thoughts left the present moment, and I projected my actions negatively into the future.

Being focused only on the outcome I wanted to achieve was not at all the mindset that had created my amazing results at Alcatraz. In fact, it was quite the opposite. For the Alcatraz race I'd taken in every moment just as it happened. I was accepting and adaptable to the present situation, however it unfolded.

Every moment was perfect in my mind because I did not have any preconceived notions about how it should be. It was just as it was, and that perspective helped to keep me in the *now*.

In the low-ropes exercise my mindset was very different. I certainly was not accepting of the circumstances that were presented to me in the moment. I could not accept that what I'd planned and envisioned is not what was happening.

We had a few days between the low-rope and high-rope days to soak up what we had experienced and think about how any insights of self-discovery applied to other areas of our lives.

Awareness is the first step in applying anything in life, leading to growth and change. It was amazing to me just how true this proved to be in the coming days. After I became aware of my lack of being adaptable to the present situation, I saw just how often this response showed up in my life. When things did not play out exactly as I envisioned, I focused on my own shortcomings and ultimately how those shortcomings would lead to failure. This attitude was harsh and also unforgiving.

## HIGH-ROPES DAY

It was the night before high-ropes day and we were all settling in for a good night's rest. There was one exercise in particular that we all knew was coming, and it was the talk of the dorms that night. Before signing up we had watched a video showing highlights of our upcoming week. The one exercise that gave everyone some level of anxiety was called The Pole. Safely harnessed and tethered to multiple lines, people in the video were shown climbing a 30-foot telephone pole capped off with a round disc of the same diameter. The goal was to step onto the top of this unstable platform using no handholds or assistance. Once standing, they turn 180 degrees and then jump from the top of the pole to catch a trapeze bar placed some 6 feet out in front of them.

As I lay in bed my mind wanted to go to "the how," namely how is this going to even be possible. What's the best strategy to approach this exercise to ensure I would catch the trapeze bar? Because, of course, nothing short of catching that bar would be success for me. And then it hit me. I stopped going down the same old road in my thought process and began to ask myself: *How am I going to apply what I learned in the low-ropes exercise to this new exercise?*

I wrote in my journal: *I know that my best strategy was to be present. To cherish each moment of the experience just as I had done in the Alcatraz race. Now I'm learning to be adaptable to whatever arises in the situation at hand. Not be fixated on a particular outcome, but to enjoy the journey as it unfolds—as I've envisioned it or not. Perfection is in the moment.*

Fast forward to the next day and my turn at The Pole. My intention was to channel my nervous energy into being present and in the moment. I told myself, *Enjoy the experience, take it all in, and remember each step.* Just as I'd done at Alcatraz, I knew I could face down my fear with a present mindset and thus fully embrace *the power of now.*

Harnessed and connected to more lines than I could count, I approached the base of The Pole. Taking a big breath, I reached up to grab hold of the first peg, pulling my body weight up as I lifted my foot off the ground. I reached for the second peg, and my other foot came up. I was off.

I climbed steadily, looking for each peg one-by-one, not breaking my focus and pulling my body up the pole. Before I knew it I was at the top. Climbing, I knew, would be the easiest part. Now I was faced with a different step. I had to hold on to the top of an unstable disk the size of a large dinner plate and somehow get both of my feet between my hands.

*Climbing the Pole*

Surprisingly, it wasn't as hard as I had expected. I was now squating on the disk atop a 30-foot pole, in a tight tuck position, hands firmly gripping the sides of the disk. My next move was to stand straight up. Only, if I did that, there'd be nothing to hold on to. As I shifted my eyes forward, I became aware of just how high 30 feet was, especially when there isn't an inch of extra room to move your feet and the fall would be a long one.

Slowly, I straightened my body to stand. As I did, my legs began to shake. *Crap! They are shaking again*, I thought immediately.

*Don't let your legs shake,* I advised myself.

They shook more.

*It's not supposed to happen this time,* I couldn't help but reprimand myself.

And then a split second later, I looked up, took a deep breath and reminded myself to be present in the now. *Enjoy this very place in time, the moment!* I saw the photographer perched in a treehouse built on the top of another pole, poised and ready to click. I saw the birds in the treetops from an angle I'd never seen trees or birds before.

*Standing on the Pole*

Suddenly, without any conscious direction, my legs stopped shaking. With my hands extended straight out to the sides like airplane wings, I began to inch my feet in a circle to the left to make the 180-degree turn, taking notice as I went of the varying colors of green leaves that made up the trees. I never realized a single tree could have so many shades of green. *That is amazing,* I recall thinking.

I continued around until I saw the trapeze bar suspended a good 6 feet away. *Geez, that sucker is out there!*

Again, I paused to take in my surroundings as I contemplated the trapeze bar. One single thought flooded my mind: *I don't have to catch that bar. I want to catch that bar.* I bent my knees and then exploded through my legs, pushing off in an outward leap as hard and as far as I possibly could. I caught the bar with one hand and the other followed suit.

*Jumping from the Pole to the trapeze bar*

I had done it!

As the crew lowered me down to the ground, I caught the eye of my partner from the low-ropes exercise and raised my arm with a celebratory fist pump. I had shared with her the lessons I'd learned and my new strategy of staying present rather than focusing on past failure.

"It worked!" I exclaimed, beaming from ear to ear.

*Me after the climb*

## REFLECTING BACK

Staying focused on being present during The Pole exercise, as well as during the Alcatraz swim, not only brought the results I wanted, but it showed me how satisfying the journey could be when I took the time to enjoy it. It also taught me that the way to create amazing results was to stay present even when things weren't going the way I expected them to go.

Unlike The Pole, during the Alcatraz Challenge, I had not encountered any game-time disappointments along the way. Alcatraz was all about staying in the moment and enjoying the journey. In the end, the execution of my plan had gone smoothly. But The Pole was about more than staying present; it was also about overcoming a previous failure and having the ability to adapt to my surroundings. First, I had to overcome the disappointment of the low-rope exercise. Next, in the high-rope exercise, I had to adapt to my situation, the shakiness of my legs, and change my approach, removing all negative self-talk. All the while reminding myself to cherish the moment, just as it was.

The Pole showed me firsthand just how quickly my thoughts could change my actions and how quickly I could adapt to the changing environment around me. My legs went from shaking uncontrollably to perfect stillness in the blink of an eye, all because I chose to think differently. All of the tools I had learned from previous experiences were coming together. When I fractured my back I chose to meet adversity by embracing new hope and took up swimming. When I swam Alcatraz I chose to face my fear by creating a new way of thinking that kept me being present and enjoying the journey.

On the pole, by combining the power of now with the choice to think positive thoughts, I was able to eliminate all distractions and swiftly adapt to the changing situation. This allowed me to reach my final destination, which was the trapeze bar, and succeed in my execution.

I realized that I used the same principles in my professional career. At the time, I helped lead my firm's strategic planning process that resulted in a business plan to serve as a guide for the coming year. When the plan is authored it is written as a working document, meaning our intent is to revisit the plan periodically throughout the year. Keeping the plan as a working document, able to be altered at any moment, allows us to stay in the present with our plan. Then, the act of revisiting the plan allows us to adapt to changing market conditions. While the goal remains the same, the plan may require some changes in course. No plan is ever perfect nor will a plan ever be executed perfectly. There must always be room for change.

Whether my goal has been personal or professional, fitness-related or business-related, my ability to remain in the present moment and adapt to changes in my environment has been one of my keys to success. The journey can bring new discoveries and often a far richer and more satisfying experience than anything I could ever have planned.

## Play #4: Deal with the Unexpected

Growing up, I always enjoyed math. It made sense to me, especially algebra which was all about equations with constants and variables—certainty and uncertainty. The same applies in life. Once you identify the elements of your state of being that work for you, you have found the fixed numbers in your life's equation. Regardless of the circumstances, you know you can rely on these fixed elements. They are certain and you know they won't change.

Variables are a different story. In math, variables are the unknown parts of the equation, the parts that we work to solve and make known. In life, variables are circumstances that arise unexpectedly. We must learn how to quickly identify and sort through the unexpected.

To be unstoppable, what works is having the ability to stay present and fully engaged. Let's call that ability a constant. It works in every situation regardless of the circumstances. To find more of your constants, you must look back on your past experiences and identify the things that worked, the things that helped you succeed and overcome unexpected obstacles. Your constants are the things that will ground you, the things that you continue to fall back on time and time again.

To be unstoppable, you must also be aware of the variables in your life, those things that are not certain, not expected. The variables are always changing as your circumstances change. While you may have a great plan for accomplishing your goal, a variable can appear unexpectedly to derail you. That's when you want to be able to fall back on your constants, the things that work for you. Now you are prepared to accept those unexpected situations and adapt your plan accordingly.

Becoming unstoppable means that you combine your ability to be fully engaged and present in the moment with your ability to deal with the unexpected. With that equation, you have a formula for success in all that you do!

# Kristy's Game Time Coaching
# Journal Entry

Recall a time in your life when you were faced with something unexpected. Describe the experience in detail.

Begin by describing your self-talk. What did you say to yourself throughout this situation? Were you positive and encouraging? Were you able to sort through your emotions and the experience, moving forward in a new direction you felt good about? What did you learn through this experience that allowed you to move forward?

Or did you find yourself stuck in your original thinking, unable to adapt to change? How did this make you feel? What was the outcome? How did you come to peace with that outcome?

Pay particular attention to your thoughts. Were you present in the moment and able to identify what showed up? How did you deal with the unexpected? How did you feel? What helped you move forward? What thoughts or actions did not help? It is equally important to identify what doesn't work as what does. By being clear on what works and doesn't work, you are armed with the knowledge necessary to quickly evaluate situations and uncover your best strategy moving forward. This will allow you to better deal with the unexpected in the future.

# CHAPTER 5

# DREAMING BIG:
# MY 90-DAY CHALLENGE

*Every great dream begins with a dreamer.*
*Always remember, you have within you the strength, the*
*patience and the passion to reach for the stars,*
*to change the world.*
—Harriet Tubman

The weeklong retreat had been eye opening. Now back at home, I was settling into my routine and eager to apply what I had learned. Within weeks, I enrolled in the next phase of the leadership course series. This next course was a 90-day program, structured to have me prove I could accomplish anything I set my mind to by applying what I'd discovered about myself during the seven-day retreat. This program was going to test my new abilities in ways that would make me stretch and become unstoppable.

The 90-day period began by setting goals that would shake my foundation, tax my sense of limits, and scare the heck out of me. My *big, hairy, audacious goals,* I would call them, to remind me that I was taking on something designed to rock my world. There were four categories of goals: physical, mental, emotional, and wealth-building. The one requirement was that each goal must stretch me beyond what I thought possible to achieve in 90 short days. If the goal didn't make me sick to my stomach just by contemplating it, it was not big enough. This program was designed to push me far beyond my comfort level. To succeed, I'd have to become comfortable in the uncomfortable—something I could barely imagine doing.

*Describing my "why" behind my goals during an interview*

Throughout the 90-day period I would be assigned a coach to provide daily support to achieve my goals, yet at the same time, challenge me from all angles. On any given day this coach could task me with an activity or an exercise intended to reveal self-doubt, defeating thoughts, or weaknesses related to me achieving my goal. On the flip side, the assigned activity could show me a strength, skill, or a characteristic I was underutilizing or denying. It was all for my growth and eventual success.

The 90-day program was intended to be intense and build upon my previous discoveries about myself. I had witnessed some of the other participants who attempted to complete the program before me struggle and drop out. Yet I'd also seen many more who were amazed at what they'd learned, and in return, were able to create new lives to step into in a short period of time. Many people did not stop after the 90 days; they took what they created and carried it forward to achieve even greater success and freedom in their lives. I wanted those results, and I was ready for the challenge.

## MY PHYSICAL GOAL

Clearly I had a history of enjoying a good physical challenge, so I thought it was only appropriate that I start with my physical goal. To get started, I sought coaching and advice from two individuals. The first was Brett, the coordinator of the 90-day program; the second was Jack, a friend whom I'd met in the leadership courses who had previously experienced success in the 90-day program. Jack, as it turned out, would be there for me throughout my entire 90-day challenge. He believed in me and saw something I'd not yet uncovered about myself. And I trusted his bigger picture perspective.

I placed a call to Brett. In helping me to define my big, hairy, audacious physical goal, Brett asked if there was anything I had always wanted to do but never thought I could. His question reminded me of the bucket list that I'd created years ago.

My mid-30s had brought about what my dad refers to as an early mid-life crisis. I went through a period of a few years where I tried to rediscover myself. What was it that brought me undying happiness—the kind of happiness that did not require searching but came easily and found its way naturally to me? As I child, I was in touch with that kind of happiness, but at some point between my late 20s and early 30s, I had lost that feeling. On a quest to rediscover it, I created a bucket list of 50 items I wanted to do in my lifetime. I thought that if I could cross them off, I just might stumble upon the kind of happiness I sought.

Now, responding to Brett's question, I thought back to that list. I had always wanted to sky dive. For certain, jumping out of a plane would be scary and not something I would choose to do every day; however, someone could just push me out of a plane tethered to another skydiver. It would be over in just minutes! Such a feat did not seem like it would take all that much of a commitment on my end. I needed something I would have to train for, something for which I had to push my body to new physical limits in order to attain.

Another item on my list was a physical challenge common to many Arizonans: hiking the Grand Canyon rim-to-rim-to-rim. Hikers either start on the north or south rim of the Grand Canyon, hike to the opposite rim, and then turn around and head back to the starting point. The challenge comes from doing it nonstop in one day, a very taxing feat. Yet I knew with a few months of training I could accomplish it. The thought of hiking the Canyon just did not turn my stomach quite enough.

Brett and I went back and forth, throwing out ideas. After each one I shrugged my shoulders and said, "Okay...." While I had not done any of them before and they were remarkable accomplishments, I was confident I could complete them. Every idea that came up would have taken work and all would have been rewarding. It was just that they didn't give me that sick-to-my-stomach feeling, and therefore didn't really qualify as big, hairy, and audacious.

Almost at a standstill, I finally hit on it. One of the 50 items I wanted to do in my lifetime was to complete an Ironman. I had always admired people who had taken on what was once considered to be the greatest human endurance race of all time – a 2.4 mile swim, a 112 mile bike and a 26.2 mile run.

Having been a marathoner, I knew the discipline and hard work it took to train for just running the 26.2 miles. I could not possibly imagine what it would be like to train for three sports in one training cycle. I was in absolute awe of anyone who had finished an Ironman and heard the words, *You Are An Ironman*, at the finish of the 140.6 mile course.

This was it. The nauseating feeling I was supposed to get—it was definitely there. I was going to do an Ironman!

As with any good plan, it's important to assess where you are starting. For me, that starting point was a pretty low rung for someone considering an Ironman. I had never entered a triathlon of any distance, and I'd never swum more than 1.5 miles. I didn't even own a bike. Sure, I'd conquered a marathon run of 26.2 miles and finished decently. But I had never finished a swim race to immediately jump on a bike and then hit the road for a run. Add to that, I had never swum or biked the distance required by an Ironman. The fact is, it is completely unheard of for a person to compete in an Ironman as their first triathlon. At least no one I knew had ever heard of anyone doing that.

I definitely had my work cut out for me.

## MY WEALTH GOAL

Next was my wealth-building goal. This goal had to be something that created financial wealth in my life. I defined *true wealth* as working at something I was passionate about. I wanted to spend my life earning a living doing what I loved, something I would do even if no one paid me to do it. I already knew my passions included sports, nutrition, overall good health, children and helping others to become more than they thought they could become, to be empowered, and successful in all that they did. Along those lines, any talk of meeting the challenge of fighting childhood obesity could get me motivated.

Even though I couldn't envision how earning a living by living my passion might look, I believed someday it would happen. But I was not ready for a career change at that point in my life. For the time being, I lived out my passion through philanthropic work and physical challenges, such as the Foundation for Blind Children and marathon goals. This always seemed to bring me a tremendous sense of satisfaction.

Seeking advice on how to structure my wealth goal, I consulted Jack, my friend who had experienced tremendous success in his 90-day challenge. He suggested I marry my two passions together by connecting my Ironman ambition to a fundraiser to combat childhood obesity, and have it all happen in a 90-day period.

This got me thinking. Completing an Ironman is an accomplishment in and of itself. Training for one in 90 days without any triathlon background, or even a bike on day one, was unheard of. I believed taking on this challenge would inspire people to support me and the cause I would be representing. I could create a fundraising campaign centered on my Ironman challenge and generate awareness about childhood obesity by collecting pledges for my race. I just needed to connect my efforts to the right organization to make it all happen.

A few months earlier, I had been introduced to Rebekah Diaz, the Executive Director of a new nonprofit in Arizona called The Action Foundation. According to their mission statement, The Action Foundation was "solely focused on increasing children's activity levels through after-school fitness conditioning and nutritional education." In talking with Rebekah, I learned they needed $35,000 to fund an after-school program teaching children about good nutrition and proper exercise. This amount would be enough to fund a yearlong program at one school, reaching 200 children. Looking back on this conversation, I knew I wanted to help provide those kids with this opportunity.

My wealth goal became clear to me. I was going to raise $35,000 for The Action Foundation to fund their first after-school program—and do it in 90 days. My vehicle to raise the money would be my physical goal of Ironman in 90 days. I would create a campaign that would soon be called Journey to Ironman Cozumel.

Rebekah and I began brainstorming how to create the campaign. Rebekah's first idea was to host a day camp called ACTION Camp, collecting registration fees for families to attend and experience the kind of offerings the foundation would feature in their year-long program. A second idea was to host a luncheon on childhood obesity featuring a guest speaker. This event would be funded by registration fees and proceeds from a silent auction. Our final idea was to host a golf tournament, which could also include a silent auction. The ideas were flowing. Together we went to work to create our campaign plan.

## My Emotional Goal

As the idea of competing in an Ironman began to sink in, I realized the thought alone of riding a bike gave me complete anxiety. I'm talking *major* anxiety. Forget the 140.6 miles—just the thought of getting on a bike, clipping my feet into the pedals, and riding while cars whizzed by at 60 plus mph was enough to make me, literally, sick.

It was completely irrational. The fear I had actually came as a surprise to me and just about everyone I told. I had never been afraid of any physical challenge. Why was riding a bike so terribly scary to me?

I thought back to the times I had ridden a bike. My first bike had a small pink frame with a white basket tied to the front of the handlebars and a bell off to one side. Beautifully displayed on the front of the basket was a set of multi-colored plastic flowers. The first day we brought my bike home, my dad installed training wheels. These small wheels aside the rear wheel only touched down if my bike began to tip.

With the slightest contact with the pavement, these wheels would bounce me back to a neutral position and save me from falling. This was great! I could ride all over the neighborhood and enjoy my new found freedom safely.

Until one day, my dad decided I was ready for the next step, to ride without the training wheels. As I watched him remove those two tiny wheels that provided such stability, it was as though he was slowly removing any confidence I had built. Nonetheless, he assured me I was ready for the two-wheel contraption. Or in my mind what looked more like a pink unstable monster sitting atop two wheels. I still have a clear vision of what happened next that day. My dad began by running alongside my bike, intervening any time I appeared unstable. Each time I felt the slightest wobble, apprehension built and I quietly prayed my dad wouldn't let go. I was so afraid of falling to the ground. Being the girly-girl I was, I wanted to avoid falling and scraping my knees at any cost. But after I outgrew that little pink bike, my memory of riding bikes disappeared – until Amsterdam.

It was in Amsterdam, as I was passing through on my way home from Kilimanjaro, that I encountered a bike again. This bike was not little, nor was it pink. In fact, it was a rental bike that was far too big for me. I had to jump completely off the seat every time I came to a stop, just so my feet could reach the ground. But even though my bike and I weren't a good fit, no trip to Amsterdam is complete without a ride through the city using this method of transportation.

Customary for Amsterdam, it was a cool, overcast day with scattered rain showers when I decided to go for a ride. With more than 700,000 bikes in the city, bike lanes are on every main road. In fact, the Dutch bike system is like no other. It is an intricate part of the public transportation system, and it might have been wise to hear a brief tutorial on the rules of the road before taking to the streets. But I didn't have time for that, so I hopped on my oversized bike and set out to explore the city.

I was riding single file in the bike lane alongside the flow of traffic when I looked up and realized that bike lanes have their own traffic lights, coordinated but separate from the main traffic signals. And the one I was rapidly approaching was red. I hit the brakes, abruptly angling my tire to avoid hitting the bike already at a standstill in front of me. This caused me to completely lose my balance and fall to the ground, bringing the entire bike down on top of me. I vividly remember hearing the ding of the bell as it hit the ground, only to look up and see the Dutch man on the bike I nearly missed looking down at me and shaking his head in disgust. I was not only hurting, but embarrassed for not knowing the rules. That was my last time on a bike.

The thought of getting on a bike again made me more than uncomfortable—but in order for me to complete my goal of doing an Ironman in 90 days, I had to overcome my anxiety and get comfortable riding a bike. My emotional goal became just that. I decided in order to overcome my fear of riding a bike, I would spend 30 or more hours riding on the main roads.

When I set my goal, I had not yet purchased a bike. My options were either a road bike or a tri-bike. I selected a tri-bike because of the unique positioning of the seat relative to the handlebars, as well as the aero bar feature (the small straight bars that extend out to the front and house the gear levers) that allows the rider to utilize different muscles while riding and thus save some of their leg muscles for the marathon. While tri-bikes are designed to make the rider more efficient, they are also known to be more difficult to ride. But I figured if I was going to do it, I'd do it right and have the best possible advantage come race day.

## MY MENTAL GOAL

My fourth and final goal was my mental goal. I was coached to choose something that would ground me, bring me to a place of inner stillness, and quiet my mind.

It does not take knowing me long to learn that I am not very good at spending quiet time, sitting still all alone with my thoughts. I would define quiet time as the time spent running or swimming. Whenever I ran alone I would problem-solve. And when I swam I would meditate, focusing on the sound of the water moving across my body. Neither of these embraces the concept of sitting still. Infact, I could not even recall the last time I actually sat down to watch television.

There was one time, a year prior, I had experienced the full meaning of inner peace and tranquility. I had just gone through a tough breakup and needed an escape. I traveled to Costa Rica for a week with my dad and his wife for a deep-sea fishing trip, one of my bucket-list items. Costa Rica is known for their world-class, deep-sea fishing and I could not think of someone more fitting to experience this with than my dad. My family had owned a lake house on Grand Lake in Oklahoma before I was even born. Throughout my childhood years, I spent my summers at our lakefront home, skiing and fishing. It was my dad and his father who taught me to fish at a very young age on this very lake.

Costa Rica was not only known for their great fishing, but they were also known for their surfing, yet another item on my bucket list. Intending to cross both off the list, I joined my dad and his wife at a small surf town called Samara along the Pacific coast. My dad found a great boat captain and crew to take us fishing for the day, and I found the perfect surf school with beginner waves nearby. What I had not planned to find was Kate, a European yoga instructor who taught yoga on the beach right next to the surf school. After asking around my first day in town, I discovered she was the best in the area and I decided to give yoga a try too.

Knowing absolutely nothing about yoga, I thought a private lesson might be the way to go. Kate proved to be the perfect teacher. She knew the right balance to push me physically yet do it in a peaceful, calming manner. She taught me how to focus on the sound of the waves crashing against the shoreline and block out all other noise. I'm not sure I'd ever felt so much at peace in my life. It was as though all the uncertainties and areas in my life that felt unbalanced were suddenly centered. Even better, I seemed to carry the feeling with me throughout my entire day. It was incredible. I finally knew what it meant to be in a meditative state. I was hooked and continued under her guidance for the entire week.

Once back in the States I searched for a way to re-create the inner peace I'd felt under Kate's guidance. I went to yoga classes at my gym only to be disappointed to discover they played music during class. The music took me away from the place of serenity I had experienced on the beach. I missed the sound of the waves and feeling as though nothing else existed. If only I could recapture my costal experience and bring that foucs into every aspect of my life, imagine how much more fulfilling life might become.

With Kate's yoga class as my only reference of what it felt like to shut my mind down, I set my mental goal around finding that tranquility I'd been immersed in on the beach. I would bring the beach home with me and make a goal to meditate for 15 minutes 60 times within the 90-day period. And it would not count if I fell asleep!

## GOING PUBLIC WITH MY GOALS

Brett, the program coordinator, encouraged me to share my goals with as many people as possible as a way to help hold me accountable for accomplishing them, and also to create a support system. I accepted the challenge and sent out an email to my friends and family members. This email would set the stage with a positive mindset as I began my journey.

To the Movers and Shakers of My World,

You are receiving this message because you have played an important role in my life at one time or another. You have been there to celebrate my success, and to pick me up and dust me off when times didn't seem as bright. Together we have shared in this amazing journey called "life." It only seems natural that I would want to share my next chapter of the adventure with you.

This past July, I took on the challenge of understanding what lies within me and how I can drive the results I want moving forward—becoming unstoppable in achieving my dreams and goals. I am now entering into a 90-day program where I set four *big, hairy, audacious goals*. These goals are meant to stretch me beyond what I think is possible, but with the right mindset, attitude, and support, I know my goals will become reality. I can already see the results!

Here are the big, hairy, audacious goals I will accomplish over the next 90 days:

- Physical Goal: Complete Ironman Cozumel 2010.

- Emotional Goal: Overcome my fear of riding a bike by riding 30 or more hours on my tri-bike on main roads.

- Wealth Goal: Raise $35,000 in 90 days for The Action Foundation to fund their first after-school program fighting childhood obesity.

- Mental Goal: To meditate 15 minutes a day, 60 times within the 90-day period.

I am sharing these goals with you to ask for your support and also to invite you to celebrate with me when they are totally blown out of the water!

Sincerely,
Kristy

## DREAM BIG – ACHIEVE GREATNESS

I always told myself I would never settle in life for something less than my dreams. Yet looking back over the past few years, I had broken that promise to myself. I had settled for things in my life, whether they were relationships or my career, because they felt good enough at the time or they were what others envisioned for my life. But that was about to turn around. I did not take on this 90-day challenge to prove anything to anyone other than myself. It was time for me to get out of my comfort zone and reach for those big dreams I'd always had. I certainly believed that anything was possible and I was committed to proving that big dreams could come true.

Entering into those 90 days of the unknown was scary yet exhilarating at the same time. Whenever someone reacted to my goals as impossible, I would remind myself that anyone who had made a discovery, invented something, or set a new record, started with a simple dream. It was a dream they believed in and could envision happening. At the time they had their dream, they might not have known exactly how to make it happen, yet they were determined and knew exactly what they wanted. They had clarity in their goal and they were committed.

For the next 90 days I was committed to embracing my dreams and creating greatness. Setting my four goals was the tool that would get me there.

## *Play #5: Dream Big and Set Audacious Goals*

Now that you have created new hope around an adverse situation in your life and new ways to think about the obstacles that stand between you and your desires, you need to be armed with new skills to create your dreams.

If you want something different, you must be and do something different. If you want to become unstoppable in life you must start by setting goals that stretch you beyond where you currently are today.

Before setting any goal, take a few minutes to get clear with your intentions. Re-read your journal entry from Chapter Two. What did you identify as your passion? What is your purpose in life? You want to make sure your dreams are in alignment with your passions. Your passion is going to fuel your ability to persevere when things get tough. And all change is hard. All change takes passion and perseverance.

Begin dreaming by letting go of what you believe is possible. Give yourself the freedom to believe that you can achieve anything. Don't hold back. Just having a dream will bring life and meaning to even the most mundane daily activities. A dream will give you something to work toward. A powerful quote from an unknown author comes to mind: *Dreams are invisible, but powerful. You cannot see them, but they keep everything going.*

# Kristy's Game Time Coaching
# Journal Entry

A. Visualize living your perfect life. What does it look like in 5, 10, 15, 20 years? Envision what you will doing, where you live, who you will share your experiences with, how you will spend your time and energy.

Write down everything you envisioned, capturing all the details. Be specific. Once you have completed your journal entry, create an image board of your dream. This can be through magazine cut outs or pictures you draw. Hang your image board where you can see it daily. Set your goals based on your dreams.

B. Next, look at areas in your life where you experience being stopped. Set some big, hairy, audacious goals to take you beyond your current limitations. Who can you put on your support team? These people will provide you feedback and guidance along the way. Stretching yourself beyond what you think is possible is the best way to break free of limitations and create a life that is unstoppable.

C. Finally, break your big, hairy, audacious goals down into bite-size pieces. Those larger milestone goals will look more manageable. As you complete the bite-size goals, you create checkpoints to ensure you are on target to meeting your larger goals. Each step of the way you will feel a sense of accomplishment and encouragement, knowing that what once looked audacious is now quite attainable.

# CHAPTER 6

# LETTING GO OF CONTROL: ADVENTURES ON THE BIKE

*Only those who will risk going too far can possibly find out how far one can go.*
—T.S. Elliot

Eighty-six days and counting to Ironman Cozumel, and my bike was finally ready to take home from the shop where I'd special ordered it. It was beautiful! The bike was special built with a frame small enough to fit my 5'2" stature, yet its vivid red color with black accents and sleek aero bars made it look powerfully fast.

Now I just had to learn to ride it.

While most people would be excited to test out such a bright new toy, I was quite the opposite. I looked for any excuse to postpone my inaugural ride. The first night was easy. By the time I got home and unloaded my bike, the sun had already set, making it too dark—at least for a novice rider—to get out on the road.

The next morning as the sun rose so did my excuses. I could feel the anxiety growing inside me. Just looking at this machine built so simply out of just two wheels, a handlebar, and a sleek frame gave me extreme discomfort. The strangest part was that there was no real justification for my anxiety. I never had a traumatic experience on a bike before, unless I counted my Amsterdam trip. While that was lingering as an unpleasant memory, it didn't seem to be the source of what had become a near-phobia. Regardless, I would have to take baby steps. I wasn't going to let my not knowing why I was so afraid stop me. To ease my anxiety I made the current day's ride just about getting comfortable and gaining some confidence.

Not yet brave enough to wear cycling shoes, I chose to ride my bike through the neighborhood wearing running shoes. At least I would not have to commit to clipping my feet into the pedals. Fearful of cars and trying to avoid as many as possible, I rode loops through my small subdivision for 30 minutes. As you might imagine, my ride was equivalent to a leisurely stroll. Only the term *leisurely* can't honestly apply since I never relaxed enough to enjoy even a single minute.

I wrote in my journal that night, "I realized how little I enjoyed riding a bike as a kid." My greatest fear had always been of cars and colliding with other riders—which is exactly what happened in Amsterdam. It was hard for me to imagine that in less than three months I'd be in an Ironman on the open road with so many other riders.

Not yet having enough confidence on my bike to complete my workouts, I had to do double duty by using the spin bike for my cardio endurance. If only a spin bike was equivalent to a tri bike, I would be right on track. I was already up to 4 hours and 9 minutes, longer than any marathon I had ever run. Couldn't I just ride the 112-mile Ironman course on a stationary bike in some nice safe spot overlooking the ocean?

While the bike training was not going exactly as planned, my running was coming along nicely. The day after my inaugural ride, I did my first 15-mile run since fracturing my sacrum. I averaged an 8:03 minute per mile pace which was encouraging. This also made for another good excuse not to ride my bike around the neighborhood later that day. My legs were just too tired from such a great run.

## GETTING ON THE BIKE

Monday, September 6, 2010, was Labor Day. The Action Foundation wanted to create a campaign video to aid in our fundraising efforts featuring me training for Ironman. Rebekah organized to have a videographer and photographer capture my training in all three disciplines: the swim, bike, and run. The short clip would be composed of interviews with my training partner, Jayson, my swim coach, Frank and me. Together we developed a campaign using the video to gain exposure. We posted the clip to Facebook and YouTube and launched an e-mail campaign to solicit donations for funding the after-school program. We later showed the video at our golf fundraiser and various speaking engagements on childhood obesity.

The biggest stress for me that day was staying on the bike long enough for the cameraman to capture what was needed and hopefully look like I at least knew how to ride. I had not gained confidence clipping into the pedals overnight, so creative film work was necessary. As it turned out, the videographer was also a cyclist and showed some sympathy towards this crazy fear of mine. He proposed a plan: He would film me on the bike clipped into the pedals and then instruct me to circle back around while he set his camera down. As I approached him I would slow down enough for him to use both hands to catch my handlebars and stabilize me, allowing me to safely unclip without the risk of falling over. No one would ever know watching the finished product how much of a novice I was.

Training became engrained in my life. Many friends and colleagues might even say it took over my life. I will admit I definitely scheduled every other part of my life around my training plans. Training was not only physically demanding but it became emotionally draining at times as well. So many emotions, fears, and personal struggles surrounded the physical aspect. My best outlet became my journal, which I wrote in every night regardless of how tired I was. Even now, reading the thoughts and emotions expressed in my journal takes me right back to that very moment. While I might not recall my fear of the bike, reading my journal reminds me of the sheer magnitude that fear had taken on in my everyday life.

The same day as The Action Foundation shot the video footage, my training partner Jayson, who was also headed to Ironman Cozumel, brought over a device called a trainer to make my tri-bike suitable for indoor riding. A typical trainer attaches the bike's back wheel to a roller base and the front wheel to a block, ensuring the entire bike will remain stable while riding. This particular block swiveled so that the handlebars could be turned to simulate the feel of riding on the road. Jayson thought the more time I spent on my bike without riding it, the more comfortable I would become. Looking back, I wish we had captured my first time on the trainer on video. I truly was starting at ground zero.

Once the bike was securely tightened into the trainer, Jayson had me climb on while he held the handlebar steady. To use the words I wrote in my journal, *I was freaked out by even that!* I begged Jayson not to let go of the handlebars for fear the bike was going to tip over. Of course this was completely irrational since the bike was securely mounted to a heavy trainer. There was no way it was going to tip or move in any direction.

Later I wrote that, as I sat on the bike pedaling very slowly, *moving my hands around or in and out of position on the aero bar seemed impossible. Yet with time, I did manage.*

Jayson instructed me to spend some time on the trainer that night and suggested the next night we ride on the road. I captured this in my journal later that night: *Jayson talked me into riding around the McDowell Mountain Loop, a big hill, tomorrow night, which literally made me sick to my stomach. I was so upset when he left, I didn't want to get on the trainer at all. However, since I promised I would, I forced myself. Within 10 minutes I was texting him from aero bar position, letting him know I was on the trainer. What was the big deal?* Looking back, I do have to laugh at my fear. However, it was very real to me at the time.

The next night Jayson arrived for our ride. However, there was no way I was going to ride on that loop with the big hill. Instead, we started out on the short block that ran alongside my house. Once again, a video camera capturing this moment would have been perfect. I can still picture that night. Me, at 36 years old, riding just one short block with Jayson running alongside me in his flip-flops, a mere repeat of my father teaching me to ride my little pink bike. Toward the end of the block, Jayson would run to the front of the bike and instruct me to brake. As the bike slowed he would grab my handlebars so I could safely unclip without the fear of tipping over. Then I would get off the bike, turn it around, and do it all over again. Up and down the block we went: me on the bike, Jayson running alongside at a slow pace. And to think—this night marked 82 days out from Ironman; 82 days until I was to ride the bike 112 miles. Trying to break the tension, Jayson remarked that he'd used the same method to teach his 5-year-old daughter to ride.

I still remember that night like it was yesterday. I stood in my driveway as Jayson climbed into his car. As he started his engine, he said to me, "I still believe in you." Then he grinned, laughed, and said, "I'm not exactly sure why, because you are not giving me a whole lot to work with … yet I really do believe in you."

That night I sat down at the dining room table to write in my journal, but just stared at my tri-bike leaning against the wall. Tears filled my eyes. I wanted to give up, to quit. Maybe all those people were right—Ironman really was an absurd goal. No one trains for an Ironman in 90 days, especially someone who'd never done any cycling before.

Finally putting pen to paper I wrote, ...*at this very moment, I am so sick to my stomach. I am so incredibly uncomfortable on the bike. Why? It's just a bike. Tons of people can ride them. Kids ride them. What is the big deal? What is my mental block?*

Still with tear-filled eyes, I used my journal as therapy. *This is the first time I seriously want to quit. I keep telling myself I felt this way when I started swimming. Yet somehow I don't seem to remember it like this. I want to sell my bike and take the $600 entry fee for the race as a loss. But I know I won't do that. What I do know is that this fear I have is not bigger than me! I will not allow it to dominate me! Maybe I need hypnosis. Anything to get over this crazy, incredible fear! What is it going to take?* I paused, and then answered my own question: *For starters, I'm clipping into the trainer. Now!*

And that is exactly what I did. I mounted my bike onto the trainer and sat on the seat for as long as it took to relax and release my anxiety. I honestly don't recall how long that took, but it did eventually happen. While this was a breakthrough, the fear didn't go away.

## EXAMINING MY FEAR

The following day I had lunch with a friend who was also new to cycling. Only unlike me, he loved riding. As I explained my fears, I remember getting irritated at even the little things, the small tokens of comforting words he attempted to give. He just didn't understand. My fears were real and I felt as though he was minimizing them. I lost my appetite. I knew the stories I had created in my mind around this bike were absolutely ridiculous. Yet no matter how hard I tried to rationalize them and tell myself they weren't real, they did not go away.

Driving away from lunch, I thought about each of my fears. First and foremost, I did not like being clipped into the bike. Clipping into the pedals made me feel too attached to the bike, as though the bike would permanently be a part of me. If I found myself in trouble, I did not trust that I could unclip fast enough. I then envisioned me tipping over, one with the bike, and crashing to the ground.

My second fear came every time the bike wobbled side to side. Wobbling was a sure sign of being out of control. I began to question if the instability of the thin tires, could actually hold me up. The slightest image of wobbling instigated yet another image of crashing. Only this image was at high speed.

Fear number three involved my gearshifts. Tri-bike gear levers are located at the end of the aero bars, not combined with the standard handlebars like on a typical road bike. Aero bars are straight bars extending out from the standard handlebars, allowing the rider to stretch into an aerodynamic position. To reach the gear lever the rider must lower to this aerodynamic position, resting forearms along the aero bars. Every time I attempted this position, the bike wobbled. I simply was not accustomed to steering with my forearms. So I chose to avoid the challenge and rode upright using the standard bars. However, this meant that every time I needed to shift, I had to let go and reach forward. Either approach resulted in wobbling. Again, I felt out of control which caused every inch of my body to be filled with fear. I just could not stop the image of crashing from entering my mind.

My last fear was of cars. Sharing the road with motorists left me feeling extremely exposed. What if they didn't see me? What if they were texting and swerved into my lane? This would be the worst crash of all. Each time a car drove anywhere near me, I could nearly feel the brush of a machine much bigger than me against my skin. I knew this would be the worst of all my fears. There is no way I would win that battle.

Having unpacked all four fears I could see that they all pointed to a fear of letting go of control. Being out of control was scary—it meant I was vulnerable. I was left exposed and susceptible to being hurt. All my life, I'd been controlling my destiny. I could control my straight A's in school by studying hard, I could control my career by delivering the work that was expected of me, I even chose relationships in which I made the decisions—control.

Control was necessary because I did not deal well with criticism. I idealized perfection in every activity I undertook and this left no room for failure. To be anything less than perfect was failure in my mind. Therefore, to give up control and to be vulnerable opened me up to criticism. It opened up the opportunity to reveal my imperfections. And that just hurt too much.

That night as I drove home, I became anxious. The closer I got, the sooner I would have to face what I had been dreading all day, which was getting on that bike. Something had to change. I was driving myself crazy, not to mention physically making myself sick.

In my desperation I remembered something I had learned in my leadership retreat. Everything is a choice, and I am the one who is making the choices. I can choose to be fearful and anxious, or I can choose to be courageous and calm. The choice is mine and, from my past experience, I knew exactly how to make the switch. It was time for me to apply what I had learned previously when facing my fears. It was time to use the power of being present in my current situation and overcome my fear of riding the bike.

I shifted emotional gears: *At this very moment I am driving home. It is a beautiful sunny day,* I told myself. As this new awareness became my focus, I could feel myself calm down. Not long after I pulled into the garage and headed to change into my cycling clothes, all the while reminding myself that all I was doing was changing my clothes. Then, as I took my bike out of the garage, I forced a smile on my face. *I am just walking with my bike,* I thought to myself. While it may seem elementary to constantly remind myself of the task at hand, it was the only way I knew to get myself to think in present terms. I had used this exercise before, whenever I was about to take on something that stretched me outside of my comfort zone, and it had worked.

Looking back I cannot recall the exact details of my ride, so I'm going to rely on my journal to describe what happened.

*Every second I felt the clips of the pedal and my heartbeat begin to climb, I brought myself back into present time. I felt the coolness of the breeze across my face, the ease of the pedals going around, the steadiness of the handlebars. I actually enjoyed my ride!*

*Conquering my bike*

*For some it may seem like a baby step, but for me it's a leap—a leap of faith, allowing myself to feel safety in the unknown, allowing myself to surrender control. I want to enjoy this feeling of satisfaction more. This ride was perfect—just how it was supposed to be!*

I recalled in my journal how excited I was at the end of my ride that I had conquered my fear this day. Getting off my bike and walking it into the garage, I thought to myself, *I should go back out and ride some more.*

And so I did. But I didn't get very far. I wrote in my journal, *As I clipped my right foot in, and it didn't seem to go as smoothly, I realized I would never be able to re-create the ride I'd just completed. I should stop, end on a positive note, and be satisfied to relish the ride I'd just taken. I had realized it was time to stop and celebrate a milestone accomplishment, not time to push for more. This was something I needed to do more often.*

I continued in my journal to say, *And the more I write, the more I'm glad I chose to stop…stop and smell the roses. Pushing is not always the best way.*

*With a smile I can say…I'm proud of myself! I'm proud I didn't give up. I'm proud I faced the biggest fear I can remember having. I know it's not over, but it is a clear breakthrough, and I'm very thankful for that.*

Closing this journal entry, I quoted self-help author Napoleon Hill: "The subconscious mind will translate into reality a thought driven by fear just as readily as it will translate into reality a thought driven by courage or faith." If that were the case, I asked myself, then *Why not think positively?*

## *Breakthrough*

My journal entries that followed over the next days and weeks continued to talk about my small rides through the neighborhood and the various thoughts that entered my mind. I was now up to 5 hours and 30 minutes on a spin bike followed by a 20-minute run on the treadmill. I was still doing double duty on the bike, taking short rides on my tri-bike to build confidence and doing my true cardio endurance work on a spin bike.

Seventy-six days before Ironman I had another breakthrough moment on the bike. That morning on a call with Ron, my 90-day program coach, I made a promise that I would finally take my bike out on the main road outside my neighborhood and not get off for 60 minutes—a ride that would definitely be out of my comfort zone. I started off and allowed myself a warm up ride through the neighborhood and around the back of the school, all familiar territory. Actually, that loop was the only place I had ridden my bike up to this point.

As I reached the intersection at the front of the school, I was stopped dead in my tracks. I recall standing there, straddling my bike, just trying to build up the courage to ride across the street. It was sunrise so there was not a single car on the road, yet it still seemed like such a big step. I compromised by walking my bike across the intersection before getting on. I will admit I continued to walk my bike across every intersection until I circled back to my house 60 minutes later.

I immediately called Ron with tearful joy announcing my success. And then I sat down to write in my journal: *It may seem small to some, however it was insurmountable to me. I literally had tears when I walked in the door. Highly emotional.*

Slowly I began to document small successes on the bike in my journal. I went from being passed by every cyclist on the road—even a local club's beginning cycling group—to catching someone on a hill. One day I wrote about being woken up by the sounds of howling winds and the immediate feeling of anxiety that followed, all because it was my cycling day. I celebrated my milestone that day by writing that I'd reminded myself, ...*fear only exists when I project into the future. So I saddled up and rode for a solid two hours. There were times it was tough, yet I still actually had fun. Shhhh...I just may be enjoying the bike.*

I noticed through my entries that I continued to focus on the positive aspects of my training, celebrating each and every sense of accomplishment. I truly seemed to cherish every aspect. Sure, I wrote about being fatigued, the pains that overcame my body at times, how overwhelmed I was fitting in work and my other goals. Yet without fail, I wrote about the gifts I had been given each and every day. I noticed that I allowed myself to see the progress I was making, even if it wasn't apparent to anyone else. This was my life, my training, and my goals. I kept my intentions clear and visualized my outcome.

Forty-five days to Ironman, and I wrote, *Had a great ride today. Completely solo and rode 100 miles! What an amazing accomplishment. Just less than 6 weeks ago, Jayson was running alongside my bike. I need to celebrate these milestones!* Although I did make note further into my journal entry that I definitely did not feel like running a marathon when I got off the bike!

I've mentioned the importance of being present and living in the moment several times. The way I overcame my fear of the bike was to not allow my mind to think about what "may" happen in the future. However, a journal entry just 13 days before my race reminds me that being present also means not living in the past.

As I began my two-week taper—the period of time before a race when it's advisable to gradually reduce mileage and intensity to allow the body to recover and rest for the big day—I wrote, *It's so hard for me not to think back to the 10 days off I took to attend another leadership retreat, the crappy workouts I had when I returned sick and the times I was convinced to cut my workouts short. Okay….this is when I need to only look forward. I can do this.*

*The past is the past. It cannot be changed. I need to make the most of every moment and allow myself to let go of those moments I wish I had done more. For some reason, at the time, I didn't do more. The decisions made then were for a reason. Believe and trust that everything has a purpose, just as it unfolds— even if it doesn't make sense.*

## ANOTHER EPIPHANY

As the days passed I became more and more comfortable on the bike. I did have to remind myself constantly to stay present, yet when I did, I was not fearful. I no longer became so worked up just at the thought of going out for a ride. Life in general seems so much more peaceful when I'm living in the moment. My bike had actually taught me a lesson that could be applied in every aspect of life. My bike was much more to me than two wheels, a handlebar, and a frame. My bike represented vulnerability, being comfortable with the uncomfortable, and feeling security in the unknown.

Knowing that like life, all the bike wants to do is stand upright and move forward.

*My bike and me... a portrait*

Living in the moment took on yet a whole new meaning to me. Like Alcatraz, living in the moment allowed me to face a fear and enjoy the journey. Yet learning to ride my bike took my understanding even further. I understood that many gifts could come from allowing myself to be vulnerable. By controlling my destiny I am actually keeping myself within the confinements of my comfort zone, the area I can control. It is when I let go of control that I enter into the unknown, become vulnerable and am exposed to new experiences and outcomes I am not able to predict. Then I have no preconceived notion of what perfection looks like, which means I am able to celebrate whatever the result may look like.

I began to take this deeper understanding into other areas of my life: my work, my relationships, and my dreams. Work became less stressful when I began to break down long-term projects into short-term milestones. Instead of being stressed that we had not landed a big job, I celebrated making strong inroads with a key decision maker or learning a key piece of information that would better position the firm. My relationships became more fruitful when I accepted them as they were and not what I hoped they would be. Instead of focusing on someone's shortcomings, or the ways in which their actions disappointed me, I looked at the value they brought to my life. I realized that no one individual could meet every one of my needs. There was beauty in having so many amazing people in my life. They each brought something different and something that added to my life.

I always had a dream of becoming a wife and mother at some point in my life. Now that I was able to embrace vulnerability, my dream looked much different. I was able to take control out of the equation. Instead of feeling frustrated that this was an area of my life where I had no control, I began to see that lack of control as an opportunity. I saw the opportunity to live as though something far more amazing than I could ever imagine was going to enter my life. I saw that vulnerability could be a good thing. While being vulnerable meant that I would open myself up to being hurt or criticized, it also meant that I could experience something greater than what I, in my mind, had ever imagined possible. Vulnerability opened me up to deeper levels of living in the now, the present moment. And if I did fall down, I knew I could pick myself up and get back on the bike.

## Play #6: Find Comfort in the Uncomfortable

We all form habits, whether it is the way we think or the way we do things. And it is only natural that we find comfort in our habits, often enforcing them by extreme control. However, when you reach for something new, a higher goal or a change of some kind, you must form new habits. This often involves some degree of discomfort.

To find comfort in something that is uncomfortable, you must allow for vulnerability. To be vulnerable means you are capable or susceptible to being wounded or hurt. While no one wishes for these things, they are a natural part of life. One of the risks of going after big dreams is the risk of not succeeding. Failing to reach a goal can be uncomfortable and hurt. But if you wish to be unstoppable, you must be confident that when you feel wounded or hurt you can shift your thinking and create new hope to then survive and flourish.

Being unstoppable does not mean you are indestructible. You will experience disappointment, hurt, and discomfort along the way. Becoming unstoppable is all about what you choose do with those feelings.

# Kristy's Game Time Coaching
# Journal Entry

Think of a time in your life when you found yourself in an uncomfortable situation. How did you feel? What new thinking did you create to feel more comfortable? What control did you have to let go of?

List as many experiences as possible and be detailed in your description. Pay particular attention to how you overcame the uncomfortable situation. This is where a shift occurred and you created new thinking, allowing yourself to find comfort with something new. How can you use your success moving forward?

# CHAPTER 7

# PERSEVERANCE: FUNDRAISER FOR THE ACTION FOUNDATION

*Promise me you'll always remember:*
*You're braver than you believe,*
*and stronger than you seem,*
*and smarter than you think.*
—Christopher Robin to Pooh

While I trained for the physical endurance I'd needed to complete Ironman, I was working hard to meet my wealth goal of raising money for The Action Foundation. Together with Rebekah, the foundation's executive director, I created a campaign called Journey to Ironman Cozumel. The campaign's mission was to provide education about childhood obesity and create exposure for the foundation's program. We would use the story of Journey to Ironman to show kids that anything was possible when you take small steps towards achieving your dreams. We had 90 days to raise $35,000, enough to fund one year of the foundation's programs.

## HOW IT ALL STARTED

I realized that every day I was reaping the benefits of being active, staying healthy, and challenging myself to push beyond the limits of whatever I thought possible. I continuously found ways to challenge myself mentally, physically, and spiritually. Countless books have been written about how good health is not just about the body, but rather comes from the mind, body, and spirit all collaborating as one. And by staying active and feeding the body to fuel activity, we serve our bodies well. While good health doesn't require that someone tackle physical activities to the extreme levels I did, I knew I could use my experiences and the lessons I'd learned from them to motivate and inspire others towards a healthier lifestyle. This became the theme of Journey to Ironman Cozumel.

Combined with my love for children, my passion was clear. When I started reading about health care reform and common health conditions that are plaguing people in the United States, I immediately saw a need. I was intrigued to learn that many chronic conditions that contribute to the majority of our healthcare deficit stem from lifestyle choices. That's right—we are making choices in the way we live our lives that are killing us! How did we ever let it get this bad? How did we allow ourselves to poison our bodies? And worst of all, why do we feel it is acceptable and continue to do it?

It seemed natural that my goal became to motivate and inspire others to make positive changes that could save their lives and the lives of their children. Through simple daily choices, dramatic results are possible. We need to focus more on education and prevention. This awareness and education component became my cause. Motivating and inspiring children by showing them that an Ironman can be conquered with 90 days of training became my driving force, and it especially sustained me when my training became overwhelming.

Rebekah and her husband, John, founded The Action Foundation purely from their passion to make a difference. Their organization's mission was to change the habits of young people and their families through the implementation of an after-school program. They started out with Saturday ACTION camps, which put kids through a variety of fun speed and agility exercises. Not only did this target the athletic kids who wanted to improve their skills, but it engaged the non-athletes and got them moving. The camp immediately received rave reviews and became widely attended.

Yet their vision was bigger. They wanted to reach more kids. They wanted to fund an after-school program which could be duplicated across the state of Arizona and eventually nationwide. The after-school program would model the ACTION camps with an added component of healthy nutrition education. They set strict guidelines for participation, including mandatory parental attendance during the nutrition component. Since parents were the ones stocking the refrigerator and cupboards or choosing to eat out, educating them was vital to the success of the program. Their vision was purely preventative by targeting elementary-aged children and their families.

I loved their vision and how big these two dedicated people were thinking. I saw how their ideas for helping kids could become viral and spread across the country. As with most start-up organizations, the missing link was funding. They lacked the funds to get the first school started. Over coffee with Rebekah I learned they needed $35,000 to fund one school's after-school program for one year, touching 200 kids. I wanted to provide this funding; I wanted to see the lives of 200 children touched and, hopefully, changed for forever!

Together, Rebekah and I crafted Journey to Ironman Cozumel, a 90-day campaign to raise the money. I quickly learned I had not only met someone who would become a lifelong friend, I had found an amazing support system. There were many times Rebekah believed in me more than I believed in myself. Little did I know at the time, but we would both take away life lessons from these 90 days.

Rebekah often referred to me as her "starfish thrower." It was a reference to and constant reminder of a story we both knew and loved about how one individual alone can make a significant difference. I include it here in its entirety:

> *Once upon a time, there was a wise man who used to go to the ocean to do his writing. He had a habit of walking on the beach before he began his work.*

> *One day, as he was walking along the shore, he looked down the beach and saw a human figure moving like a dancer. He smiled to himself at the thought of someone who would dance to the day, and so, he walked faster to catch up.*

> *As he got closer, he noticed that the figure was that of a young man, and that what he was doing was not dancing at all. The young man was reaching down to the shore, picking up small objects, and throwing them into the ocean.*

*He came closer still and called out "Good morning! May I ask what it is that you are doing?"*

*The young man paused, looked up, and replied "Throwing starfish into the ocean."*

*"I must ask, then, why are you throwing starfish into the ocean?" asked the somewhat startled wise man.*

*To this, the young man replied, "The sun is up and the tide is going out. If I don't throw them in, they'll die.*

*Upon hearing this, the wise man commented, "But, young man, do you not realize that there are miles and miles of beach and there are starfish all along every mile? You can't possibly make a difference!"*

*At this, the young man bent down, picked up yet another starfish, and threw it into the ocean. As it met the water, he said, "I made a difference to that one!"*

—Adapted from The Star Thrower by Loren Eiseley, 1907-1977

## CREATING THE CAMPAIGN

Rebekah and I both had corporate marketing and nonprofit fundraising experience. I had served as the fundraising director while sitting on the board of directors for the Junior League of Phoenix, as well as for the Foundation for

Blind Children. Along the way I had served on numerous fundraising committees for various charities around Greater Phoenix. Raising money was not a foreign concept to me.

With my career in full swing, I was working for an international architecture and engineering firm, overseeing their business development, marketing, and public relations for the Southwest region. Now joining my expertise with Rebekah's corporate marketing, branding, and social media experience, we were ready to roll.

We did realize that raising $35,000 in 90 days was an ambitious goal in any economy, let alone in the times we lived. It was 2010; companies were downsizing and corporate giving was reduced if not eliminated altogether. We definitely had our work cut out for us.

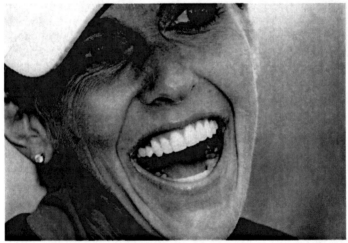

*Interview for my campaign*

We put our corporate hats on and within days we had a plan. We were first going to hold a Saturday ACTION Camp that would expose families to The Action Foundation's format, including a nutrition education component. Essentially this was a hybrid of what they had already created for this after-school program. While kids ran through an obstacle course, their parents would complete a boot camp run by my friend Ann. Ann ran an early morning boot camp and was willing to donate her services in hopes that she could attract new adult members to her program. The two camps—one for kids and the other for parents—would come together at the end of the event for a talk with a nutritionist. While we did not set a specific financial target for this event, our primary objective was to gain exposure for The Action Foundation and help to pave the way for future fundraising events.

For our second event, we planned a luncheon at an exclusive, private country club in Scottsdale where we projected to raise $15,000. We planned to hold a silent auction for the first hour and allow guests to mingle. Rebekah and I would serve as the speakers during lunch. I would talk about my Journey to Ironman Cozumel, and Rebekah would talk about the Foundation's effort to fight childhood obesity through activity and nutritional education.

For our third and final event, we would host a golf tournament projected to raise the remaining $20,000. The golf tournament monies would come through sponsorships and registration, as well as a silent auction held at a reception following the play.

We set dates, secured facilities, and signed all the contracts within a matter of weeks. The best part: each event was targeting a different audience.

We designed the ACTION Camp for the widest audience. We priced the camp low enough so just about anyone could afford to attend and marketed it to families already connected to the program, as well as Ann's existing boot camp clients. In addition, Rebekah was confident she could tap into her local radio connections, spreading the word in an effort to attract area families.

We planned to send the silent auction/luncheon invitations to both Rebekah's circle of friends and my own. These would be people we knew well personally, many who were philanthropically minded. And finally, the golf tournament would target our professional contacts, people who often golfed and worked in companies that saw the benefit of taking clients out on the course for a day.

What could possibly go wrong with our plan? It was now just a matter of execution.

We began executing all three projects simultaneously. We knew we could not do it all between the two of us, so we developed committees and committee chairs, empowering people who volunteered to direct their respective events. We, of course, kept ourselves involved to ensure goals were met and branding was consistent.

## EVENT #1—ACTION CAMP

Our first event, the Saturday ACTION Camp, did not go smoothly. We continued to run into one obstacle after another. Yet we pushed on, not altering our vision. It was logical, well thought through, and completely doable. Rebekah had experience setting up ACTION camps and Ann was already teaching daily boot camps. The formula was there and we believed that all we had to do was follow it.

Due to scheduling circumstances outside our control, we had to move our first date. With the new date finally secured, we later discovered a last-minute issue with the venue that wasn't going to work for us, so we decided to change the location. But finding another location proved to be difficult. This put our entire marketing campaign on hold. How could we promote an event, when we didn't yet know where it would be held?

After weeks of searching, we secured what seemed to be the ideal location. The only problem now was we were only one week away from our event. How were we going to get enough exposure in such little time to draw the kind of crowd we knew we needed to fill the field? Both being optimists, Rebekah and I had faith it would come together. We put our noses to the grindstone and stayed the course, utilizing every possible marketing tactic and connection we knew.

It was an extremely hectic time. I was training 30 hours a week and holding down my full-time job. I also had my daily coaching calls that brought additional challenges or assignments from my coach, Ron. I barely had the time to keep everything going, let alone deal with any problems. The need to plan and re-plan this event so many times became extremely cumbersome and stressful. Just when I thought I'd crossed something off the list, a new obstacle would arise to put it back on.

My life literally was work, training, and fundraising at this pace for 90 days. I would fall into bed every night and typically sleep soundly, but never feel fully rested when my alarm went off the next morning. Yet as tired as I was, it wasn't uncommon for me to wake up somewhere between 12:30 and 1:00 a.m., thinking about what I had to do the next day. I wouldn't fall back asleep until 3:00 or 3:30 and then my alarm would sound between 4:00 and 4:30 a.m. Not only did I train in the early morning, but on many days I would do a second workout after work.

The day of the ACTION Camp finally came. It was picture perfect: a beautiful, sunny Arizona day, an energetic DJ played bass-bumping music, a challenging yet fun obstacle course staged on a huge soccer field, booths, banners, and colorful balloons flying high. Everything was set and all volunteers were ready to go. I think Rebekah and I had enough energy to carry the entire team. *This was going to be great!*

Registration time approached. But as we waited for a line to form at the table, not a single person appeared. "That's okay," we told each other, comforting ourselves with the excuse that everyone always waits until the last minute to arrive. The cars would start rolling in and the lines would fill up any minute, right? Rebekah and I nervously shuffled things around, pretending to be busy with the final arrangements.

Starting time was quickly closing in and still no one. A close observer could see the panic setting in—Rebekah and me off to the side in a quiet conversation with beads of sweat beginning to glisten on our foreheads. Our usual happy nature was rapidly deteriorating into forced, we've-got-this-covered smiles. Scattered thoughts were running through my mind: *Had we failed? Were we not going to have one single attendee? Not raise one single penny? How could this happen? Were we not well-educated, successful businesswomen…with a plan? WOW! This just doesn't happen. And especially not to us!*

The moment had come when I could no longer deny our failure, and I felt as though everyone knew. There was no way to hide the fact that the only cars in the lot had been there since the early hours and the fields were absent people. As we looked around all we saw were volunteers slumped over completely bored. We were at a complete loss for words. I'm sure we were each searching for a scapegoat, someone we could blame, some reasonable story we could tell to spin everyone's lost time and hard work into a positive. Frozen in our places, we had to come up with something.

I'm not quite sure who made the first move but somehow we began to proceed as if nothing happened, as though everything were exactly as we had planned it. Perhaps we were able to pull off denial. We ran all the volunteers through the workout, the younger kids through the obstacle course and closed by thanking everyone profusely. As we cleaned up, we kept our heads held high; at least as high as we could to cover up. Yet, secretly, inside we were deflated.

Rebekah and I exchanged a few text messages throughout the day attempting to cheer each other up but nothing seemed to lift my spirit. Sure, I had heard of fundraisers not meeting projections and there are some that end up in the hole, but I do not think I had ever heard of one that didn't raise a single dollar.

I think it may have taken us a good day of looking really hard to find the silver lining. The lesson we agreed to take from the experience is there are times in life that holding steady to the course when all of the signs around you are telling you to take the detour, is not the answer. Strength, determination, perseverance, and positive thinking are great characteristics to possess, but they are not always the right answer. I believe flexibility to adapt to the changing environment was the one element we missed.

It reminded us both of the parable of the floodwaters.

> *As the floodwaters rose, residents were told to evacuate. One man chose to stay despite the advice of experts, friends, and family. He said he had faith in God and prayed that God would provide him answers.*
>
> *The water levels rose to the foot of his house. A rescue boat appeared. He refused to climb aboard. "No. God will provide," he said.*
>
> *The water continued to rise, forcing him to his rooftop. A helicopter arrived. Again, he refused assistance, saying, "God will provide."*
>
> *Soon the waters washed him away. Reaching the Pearly Gates, he was met by God. The man immediately questioned God, "I had faith in you. I believed you would provide for me. Why didn't you save me?"*
>
> *God replied, "I did. I sent a boat for you. I brought you a helicopter. Yet you refused them all."*

After sharing this story and talking things through, we both realized that, regardless of our spiritual beliefs, life does not always play out exactly as we envision. There is not a greater power that will make things happen for us just because it is what we want. We learned that we must yield to the signs the universe gives us, which will always direct us to safety. While having a plan is important, finding flexibility in the plan to adapt to unforeseen changes is critical.

## EVENT #2 – THE LUNCHEON

Shaking off what felt like an embarrassing failure, Rebekah and I agreed to learn from the experience and put the past behind us. We had a luncheon quickly approaching that we now needed to be our primary focus. We could not afford to have a room partially filled, so we made sure our committee felt empowered to sell group tables. Aside from the money, we knew the importance of branding and felt it was critical to the future success of The Action Foundation to pull off a successful event.

The timing was unfortunate. Just weeks after empowering our committee, I was scheduled to leave town for a 10-day woman's leadership seminar, an optional conference offered through the same leadership company I was working with. Like the other seminars, I was allowed no outside communication during this time. The day I returned, I received a phone call from Rebekah.

"I think we should pull the plug on the luncheon and cancel while we're still ahead," she said unhappily. "We just haven't sold enough seats." She felt it would be more damaging to the Foundation if we only had a few attendees. While I concurred with her assessment that a small turn out was not what the Foundation needed in order to gain momentum or branding,

I also questioned if she was overreacting and playing it safe based on what we had just gone through. Still with open wounds myself from the ACTION Camp event, I lacked the confidence to go against her wishes.

Nevertheless, my heart sank. How were we going to replace the $15,000 we projected this event to bring in?

I could choose to be upset or I could look at the opportunities still available. I chose the latter. We could continue to move forward and be able to focus all of our energy on the golf tournament. The silent auction items we had secured for the luncheon would not be a complete waste; we could easily roll them over for use in the silent auction to be held at the golf tournament. While reluctant, I was fearful of a repeat occurrence of the ACTION camp fiasco if I resisted reading the signs. I felt I needed to suck up my pride, listen to my surroundings, and embrace this unexpected change. I agreed to cancel the luncheon.

Rebekah immediately placed a call to Molly, a friend we had hired to help plan this event. Molly runs an event-planning business focused on helping nonprofits host fundraisers. She was also a member of a very exclusive club in Scottsdale which was our link to hosting the event at that venue. What happened next I could not have foreseen in a million years. Rebekah called me back, baffled and looking for advice. Molly nicely explained to Rebekah that her typical contract stated that a $500 nonrefundable deposit was required prior to any event. She further explained that she did not have us sign the contract because she understood The Action Foundation was a start-up organization and because of her relationship to me. Typically the $500 deposit would be applied toward the cost of the event. However, since we had chosen to cancel the event, we would now need to pay her $500.

I realize in the grand scheme of things $500 is not a lot of money. However, at the time it felt like a huge blow. Not only had we failed at two fundraising events and not secured a single dollar towards our $35,000 target, we were starting $500 in the hole. This just seemed to hit me hard. I questioned my friends' actions. Did friendship not supersede money? This was a start-up organization with no funds lying around. Rebekah was working for free, out of the love for the cause. I was a volunteer. And no dollars had been spent. There were no charges imposed by the venue for us having cancelled. It just did not seem fair.

Putting our feelings aside, we paid the money and had faith that we made the right decision, even if it caused us a monetary loss. I should also note that we were told we could use the $500 toward a deposit of a future event should we want to hold something in the spring. Of course this would be past our 90-day campaign deadline. Looking toward the bright side, we agreed that perhaps we could throw a spring fundraiser and begin a campaign for the next year to fund a second school. It was a great idea which raised our spirits momentarily.

Strike two and now feeling equally defeated, yet for different reasons, we had to move on to event number three. Surely we would not strike out in that effort. The pressure was now on to raise the entire $35,500 through one single event, our golf tournament.

## EVENT #3 – THE GOLF TOURNAMENT

There was one week in our fundraising campaign in particular that I will never forget. On a Monday morning at 5:00 a.m., I placed my daily scheduled 10-minute call to Ron. The focus of that day's coaching call was to remind me that midnight that coming Friday night marked day 30 of the program. I was to have a third of all of my goals met. Ron quickly transitioned into a review of the status of all of my goals. Physical...check, mental...check, spiritual...check, wealth...negative $500! He informed me I must have $12,000 by midnight Friday if I was going to have any hope of meeting that goal.

This was not exactly how I wanted to start my Monday morning. I was already feeling low enough given the two strikes. Now how exactly was I supposed to raise $12,500 in five days? (Keeping in mind I must replace the $500 I was in the hole.) My golf tournament wasn't for another 52 days.

Ron started throwing out suggestions. "Sell foursomes, sell sponsorships," He brainstormed.

*Great*, I thought. However, because we had shifted gears and placed all of our energy in our luncheon, we were behind schedule in finalizing our sponsorship package. I was still waiting on a draft from Rebekah, which left me without any marketing materials. Every good marketer knows you need a marketing package complete with sponsorship levels, benefits, and background on the charity before making an "ask."

Ron challenged my thinking. "Really?" he replied when I recapped the situation for him. He started naming off countless people he knew who were avid golfers with philanthropic hearts, none of whom, he said, would require marketing materials to commit.

This was definitely forcing me into some new thinking. Working in a large company, I was very accustomed to following protocol. And protocol definitely would have been to create the appropriate marketing materials before meeting with any prospective donor. But given my circumstance I had no other choice but to operate completely outside my comfort zone. I told Ron I'd try his suggestion and wrapped up the call.

*Interview during training*

A couple of hours later I called Rebekah. "This is my new approach—cold calling," I explained. She, too, was now being forced outside her norm. Luckily, we could both muster up a do-whatever-it-takes mentality and agreed between the two of us to pound out the calls. I was determined to not stop until we reached the goal of $12,500.

I made my first call to a friend and counterpart in my industry. I knew he played in just about every golf tournament in town. It was a perfect venue for him to entertain his clients. To my surprise he answered my call on the second ring.

After telling him about the tournament and the fundraiser he did not hesitate. "Sure," he said. "How much?"

I told him $500 for a foursome. A foursome is a package price for four golfers, ensuring they play together on the same team. As is common to most tournaments we offered a discount to register a foursome as opposed to four individual players. Not only does this fill space quicker but it eliminated the need to pair golfers.

Much to my dismay he replied, "Really? I wish it was more because I could easily charge the expense without my firm questioning a thing."

My next question was obvious, "How much expense could you charge?"

With complete confidence he tells me, "At least $1,000."

"Done!" Completely off the cuff I made the decision right then and there that a foursome along with a hole sponsorship would be $1,000. Together we agreed that in addition to the foursome, his firm would also have a hole sponsorship, an opportunity to advertise his company by placing a sign at the tee box of one of the 18 holes along the course.

Sold! This completely changed my thinking. If I sold hole sponsorships for $1,000 over merely selling $500 foursomes, I could meet my goal even faster. I began calling everyone I knew. Through a combination of $500 foursomes and $1,000 hole sponsorships, the numbers were steadily climbing. Each rejection only fueled me more to increase the number of calls. Between Rebekah and me, we had a growing number of "asks" pending.

Unfortunately, in the final days as the deadline approached many of our "asks" were coming back as rejections or those just unable to commit by our Friday deadline to raise $12,500. Stress levels were rising, yet we pulled together to come up with as many connections to golfers as we could. Still our resources were becoming exhausted. I was struggling to think of more people to ask. As I continued to think creatively of a way to meet my deadline, I thought about fronting the money myself. However, we were not allowed to contribute to our own fundraiser.

That Friday I was working feverishly between work meetings and still finding the time in the early morning and evening hours to get in my training. That night I was headed north to Bartlett Lake for my open water swim. The lake is far enough outside the city limits and drops far enough down into a canyon that I knew I would lose cell reception. On the phone until the very last minute, I had to ask my training partner, Jayson, to pull off to the side of the road so I could finish my last call before I lost service.

"Yes! Another $500!" This made taking the time for my swim slightly more palatable.

After the swim at 7:00 p.m. I realized I was only $500 away from the goal of $12,500. I told myself, *There is no way I'm coming up short now!* With several calls out I wondered who else I could reach that late on a Friday night. I was at a loss. As the night grew dark so did my chances of placing more calls.

It was 8:30 p.m. and my phone rang. It was Aaron, a guy I admired who knew the pressure I was under because he had gone through the same 90-day program years ago. I had completely forgotten about the message I'd left him much earlier in the week.

Aaron apologized for the delay in returning my call. He explained that he was out of town and driving home from a funeral, of all things. My heart sank. No matter how badly I wanted to reach my goal, I wasn't about to ask someone who'd just suffered a personal loss to make a financial commitment. But it turned out I didn't have to. I had apparently already explained my situation in a voice mail I'd left him.

He proceeded to inform me that, unfortunately, he never played golf. Yet, he seemed to have another idea in mind when he called. He then turned the question around on me. "What else would you offer for a $500 contribution?"

Unable to think quickly enough and much to my surprise, I responded with, "You tell me? What value do you place on $500, and is there something you have always wanted that I could offer you?" I should have known he would have an answer prepared.

"As a mater of fact, I've always wanted to complete a triathlon …" he replied. "Can you write me a training schedule for $500?"

I think I may have laughed, if not out loud, inside for sure. Was he serious? He wanted me…to coach him? He knew I had never even entered one myself! I could not even call myself a triathlete, let alone a coach.

In the spirit of full disclosure I reminded him of my limited background. He confidently acknowledged that he was well aware of what he was paying for and was still completely serious. He knew of my many other accomplishments and felt comfortable that I would soon be able to call myself a triathlete with the title of Ironman. He also felt confident that I could help get him in shape to complete a shorter distance triathlon, an upcoming goal.

So with a leap of faith I agreed. Done! I had successfully reached the promised amount of $12,500—even covering that $500 expense. Even if no one else remembered, I would.

With a sigh of relief I had done it. I had reached the one-third mark in all of my goals with a few hours to spare. I slept well that night.

More important than reaching my 30-day goal, I learned a valuable lesson that week which actually helped fuel me for the next 60 days. Things do not have to look perfect before I can take action. It was amazing to me what I was able to create out of nothing in just one short week. Typically I would have used that week or possibly longer to create pretty pages for a marketing package that outlined the who, what, when, and where of the golf tournament, listing the sponsorship levels and benefits. I would not have made a single call until all that was complete. But I'd been willing to think outside of the box and take Ron's crazy sounding suggestion. My ability to persevere in spite of what looked like a complete wall made me unstoppable.

## Playbook

### Play #7: Learn, Adapt, and Grow

Where it may feel like one path ends, another will appear. Perseverance is about the willingness to look for the new path. It is staying steadily persistent in a course of action or purpose in spite of difficulties, obstacles, or discouragement. Pursuing big dreams is hard work. You will encounter obstacles; however, those willing to push beyond are those who succeed. It is through perseverance you will overcome disappointment and perceived failures, and realize each experience's hidden treasures.

Pushing beyond obstacles takes courage. You must pose the courage to know when to find a new path and the courage to take it. "Courage does not always roar. Sometimes courage is the quiet voice at the end of the day that says, 'I will try again tomorrow,'" quoting from an unknown source.

Each day you have the opportunity to stay the course and drive toward the things you desire most in life. Through your actions you will either reinforce the way things currently are or you can demonstrate the new possibilities. It is all about learning from your experiences, adapting to new possibilities, and growing toward your future. When you are living with purpose you will be armed with perseverance and thus be unstoppable.

# Kristy's Game Time Coaching
# Journal Entry

Think of a time when you were derailed from a goal. How did you react? Did you stick to your roadmap and stay the course? What was the outcome? How was the journey? Enjoyable or difficult?

Or did you stop, learn from the experience, adapt your course, and grow in moving forward? What did it take for you to change your plan and create a new roadmap? What was the outcome? How was the journey?

Pay particular attention to your reactions and the behaviors that followed. What worked well for you and what didn't? How can you apply what you learned in your life moving forward?

# CHAPTER 8

# CONNECTING TO A CAUSE: IRONMAN COZUMEL 2010

*Start by doing what's necessary; then do what's possible; and suddenly you are doing the impossible.*
—Francis of Assisi

The days and months of holding down a full-time job, heading up a major fundraising campaign, and still managing 30 hours a week of training were nearing an end. I had now entered the final countdown with only seven days left to Ironman Cozumel. Yet I had still not even been a spectator at any triathlon. I had been so focused on training for the three sports that I had not given proper attention to what it was like when they were put together into a single event.

As luck would have it, Ironman Arizona was held in Tempe the week before my race. Many Arizona athletes were participating, which made being a spectator that much more enjoyable, especially since I knew some of the athletes personally. I rose early to head down to Tempe Town Lake to watch the race with some of my friends. Only I am fairly certain I watched from a different perspective than the majority of the spectators. I watched the faces of the athletes for their emotions, some in agony, some in pure joy, some in exhaustion, and some full of energy.

I clearly remember looking at my watch and noticing I'd been watching the race for more than 12 hours. My feet hurt and I was exhausted. Selfishly, I made my way back to my car and headed north toward home before many of my friends ever crossed the finish line. I was leaving for Cozumel in three short days and, at some point, I needed to remember that sufficient rest was the most important final ingredient for my race.

Before going to bed I wrote in my journal, *I am still uncertain if I am excited, nervous, or just plain scared. I was tired just watching the Ironman Arizona. In fact, as I'm writing, I realize I drove 30 minutes, had dinner, went to the grocery store, and got ready for bed—all while people I know are still out there racing. Oh my gosh!*

*I think when I picture a perfect race tonight in my meditation, it's going to look like one in which I'm having fun and smiling. That's perfection. Oh…and crossing the finish line to hear the announcer say, 'Kristy…you are an Ironman!'*

The next morning I awoke with the race still on my mind. It is highly probable that my mind had actually never taken a break from Ironman.

Later that day I received a letter that was postmarked as originating from the leadership retreat I had taken four months prior in July. One of our final exercises at the retreat was writing a letter to someone expressing all we had learned that week. After writing the letter we were told to cross out the name it had been addressed to and write in our own. Little did we realize when we started, we had just written a letter to ourselves. The facilitator promised it would arrive on a day we needed the message most.

Walking from the mailbox with the letter in hand, I could not help but grin. I wondered what I'd written. Eagerly I opened the envelope and read my own words: *Perfection is whatever is present. This very moment is perfect just as it is.*

I had written those words four months ago during my one week retreat and yet it was the perfect message for me in my final days before the race. An Ironman is an endurance race stretching up to 17 hours and anything can happen. While I had been visualizing how I would like my race to progress, I needed to remember to stay present in the face of the unexpected. This would be a tremendous mental exercise for me to stay not only focused in the present but also hold a positive mindset when it got painful and walking to the finish line, not running, seemed like a better idea.

Now just five days out from the race I received another note, this one from an anonymous member of my 90-day team:

*I see you as the enormous success that you so totally are! In all areas of your life. I'm smelling the sweet flowers and the ocean of Cozumel – seeing vast beaches, palm trees, brilliant colors, the beautiful tropical ocean of which you are a physical part of in your swim. I'm feeling the gentle breeze of air on your face that you generate on your bike ride, I'm feeling the physical sensation of sweet discomfort in your body as you challenge yourself along the scenic landscape. I see you present in joy and expectation all the while taking everything into your heart imprinting moments of your extraordinary adventure.*

*You are creating the amazing story of Kristy, a story of unconditional love for herself and others. Your ripple extends far beyond what your eyes can see. Know that your light is a huge and a welcome guide for all who are touched by you, directly or indirectly! Thank you for bringing me into your ripple! You've already won!*

And finally, the day before I left, came a note from Ron, my 90-day program coach:

*Kristy,*

*You have trained harder than anyone I know. You have more focus than most world-class athletes. You have more power than any football player. The only people that should be fearful this Sunday are your competition.*

*Based on all that you've shared with me these past ten weeks, I know that you will not only finish with your arms raised, you will do better than you can even imagine. Bring us all into your race with you Sunday morning. I will bring my running energy into your marathon.*

*You are remarkable!*

*Coach Ron*

## BAGS PACKED AND PASSPORT IN HAND

Thanksgiving morning that year had a very different feel. Instead of getting ready for a feast with family and friends, I was headed to the airport. This Thanksgiving marked my departure day. I was three days out from the race and it was time to lug my suitcase and bike to the airport.

My good friend Jack postponed the start of his holiday celebration to meet me in the airport long-term parking garage to help carry my bags, get me checked in, and see me off. At his suggestion we met early so we could sit in Starbucks and visit for awhile. He gave me such great energy and the most amazing send off I could have ever envisioned. In the final few minutes before heading to my gate, he pulled out a sealed greeting card I was to open the morning of race day. He also handed me a Jack of Hearts playing card to carry in my jersey back pocket, a reminder of his constant voice of good luck throughout the race. Jack then proceeded to tie a red ribbon around my wrist. I recognized it as the ribbon from a journal I'd given him as a gift—the same journal he'd taken to his own leadership retreat when he went through the series. And now this red ribbon was to represent his presence with me on the Ironman course.

Tears filled my eyes. I knew that every time I looked at this simple red ribbon during the race, it would remind me of his energy, words of wisdom, and positive outlook. It would remind me of why I was doing this and that I was not alone. It seemed that everything I did from this moment forward was somehow significant in ways far more apparent.

Deciding to sign up for Ironman Cozumel only a few months before race day, coupled with the fact that it was a holiday weekend, meant flights to Mexico were already filled at the time I booked mine. In order to travel on the day that best coordinated with my race schedule, I had no option but to fly first class and use the few airline miles I had left. The practical side of me was disappointed. I could have used those points for two free trips somewhere in the United States. But now as I settled into my roomy window seat, spending the extra miles didn't seem quite so bad.

As I sat alone that Thanksgiving morning, I remember gazing out as we sat on the ground. I don't recall all the thoughts that went through my mind, but I do recall being so overwhelmed with emotion that I pulled out my journal and wrote the following: *My life is so blessed and so full of amazing people. I have so much to be grateful for today. I give thanks for everything— all the important things in life. I am abundant. Not because I am physically surrounded by loved ones, however, because I feel full of love, joy, friendship, strength, and life purpose. For that, I give thanks.*

I may have been physically alone that Thanksgiving, but I felt the support and comfort of all those who believed in me. They surrounded me that moment on the plane and little did I know how much they would continue to give me strength when I needed it most.

Just as I promised myself I would, I cherished every moment in Cozumel leading up to the big day. My days were far busier just preparing for the race than I'd expected. Getting my bike put back together after the flight, picking up my race number from the expo, attending the athletes' meeting, packing everything I would need in all of my transition and special needs bags, ensuring I had all of my nutrition on my bike and in the correct bag for the appropriate time in the race—all that and I'm sure more. In that brief time before race day, my mind never moved far from Ironman.

## NOVEMBER 28, 2010 – RACE DAY!

I awoke just seconds before my alarm went off, popped out of bed and grabbed my swimsuit and the special triathlete shorts I would wear to the race start. Once dressed, I peeled open the envelope of Jack's card. I had been eagerly waiting the moment I could read his words of wisdom, and that moment had finally come.

*Good morning, amazing one!*

*Today is your day. Do you feel the love all around you? It is everywhere! It is being sent to you from so many people—family, friends, the universe, and most importantly me. Take time this morning to hear my voice reminding you of how amazing you are, how hard you have trained, how great you are, what an amazing athlete and woman you are. Your experience will be everything it is supposed to be today, and it will be amazing!*

*Just be you and take it all in. Feel the support of the water hugging you like a friend on the swim, hear the wind on your bike whispering words of encouragement and support, touch the red ribbon on your wrist and connect with your heart on the run, and know how much you are loved.*

*Like always, I will have you in my heart all day. This day is yours. The race will be what you make it. Surrender to your greatness and have an amazing experience.*

*All my love,*

*Jack*

I headed downstairs to the hotel lobby just before 5:00 a.m. Walking through the lobby dressed only in my swimsuit, tri-shorts, and flip-flops, I actually felt as though I was forgetting something. How could I possibly be ready to take on those 140.6 miles packed so light? Something must be missing! I had to reassure myself that the rest of my gear, and my bike, would be at the appropriate transition areas. As required by all athletes, I had dropped off my gear bags during the bike check-in just yesterday. It was up to the race officials to get them to the appropriate transition areas. Now on the morning of the race I felt the tremendous trust that was required, something completely new since I had never completed a triathlon. When I ran marathons I showed up to the start line with everything I needed. This was new territory. Yet, then again, I was about to enter into a full day of new experiences.

I had two gear bags, one for the transition between swim to bike and the other for bike to run. My bike gear bag contained a jersey and bike shoes along with helmet and other necessities, such as sunscreen and sunglasses—essentially everything I would need during the bike portion of the race. All of my nutrition was already packed in a pouch strapped to my bike's straight bar, allowing me to consume sufficient calories every

45 minutes. The day before I had lined the pouch with several gel packs which would provide me instant energy without needing to chew. I also slid in my Jack of Hearts card along the side, just another reminder of Jack's encouraging words.

*Checking my bike in at the transition area*

During an Ironman, an athlete never stops to eat. One must learn to eat on the bike as well as on the run. I did prefer to have some solid food about half way through the bike course. My choice was a half a peanut butter and honey sandwich, which I stuffed into the back pocket of my bike jersey. My run gear bag contained similar gear but with a sun visor, running shoes, and a body glide stick for relief from possible chafing caused by clothing. It also contained sunscreen and more nutrition, including a banana and another half a peanut butter and honey sandwich that I would quickly devour while I was changing shoes and on the way to the start of the run course.

Once outside the hotel, I found the cab I arranged to take me to Chankanaab National Park, the start of the race. Once on-site, my first stop was to check my bike to see how the tires had held up over night. They actually weren't too bad but I decided to top them off with a little air from another competitor's hand pump. My next stop was to locate my bike gear bag. We were told this area would not be open to us prior to the race start but I saw several people making their way over. So I followed along. It wouldn't hurt to see what row my bag was hanging in so I could find it easier once out of the water. I was quite eager for the race, which explained why I arrived so far ahead of the other athletes. But my nerves also created constant urges to use the restroom, which consisted of port-a-potties, a necessity for any outdoor endurance event. I must have made three trips over the course of 45 minutes.

The time had come to head down to the pier where I would enter the ocean with the other athletes and tread water until the gun sounded, indicating the start of Ironman Cozumel 2010. As I stood among the other athletes I watched the dolphin show, typically a tourist attraction but today part of the opening ceremonies for the race. Crowds of spectators lined the pier and enjoyed the show that came just before the start for the professional athletes, which was earlier than the rest of us. Of the 2,800 competitors, a handful were professionals triathletes who were racing for prize money. They were customarily given an early start time to avoid having to fight the crowds of amateurs like me.

After the dolphins submerged below the surface of the water, we began the walk down the long dock to enter the water. For some reason I wasn't at all nervous. I just felt calm and very present.

## THE SWIM

Once I entered the water I still had 10 minutes to tread before the amateur's gun time, announcing the start of the race. It was as though I floated effortlessly, buoyed up by my excitement and the excitement of everyone around me. When the gun sounded, I estimate I was mid-pack among the swimmers. I had no idea where to position myself so as to avoid bumping into others. In running marathons—my only real experience up to this time with exception of Alcatraz—the runners line up in corrals based on their projected finish time. This puts the faster athletes up front and keeps the flow moving. Faster runners don't have to dodge slower runners and slower runners don't get run over. Since this was a water start, I had no idea where I should line up. If I went too far to the outside, I'd have to swim farther to get around the buoys; if too far to the inside, I'd have to fight my way back to stay to the outside of the buoys. Since there is no way to corral a water start, swimmers typically have no idea of the pace of the swimmers around them, and it feels rather chaotic.

There were so many people around that I knew it would be impossible to get totally out of the way. In open water swim races people will literally swim over the top of other swimmers, causing the person on the bottom to feel as though they were being drowned. Since I'd never done a triathlon, let alone an open water start, I'd been left only to hear the horror stories other triathletes told, and I'd been warned that some would swim at any cost. If they don't go over you, but instead swim beside you, they can get so close that their elbows and hands knock your goggles completely off.

Luckily I didn't experience any of these things. But I definitely experienced some aggressive swimmers that came straight at me, attempting to cut me off and push me out of the way. And I did get hit in the face and body several times. But what could I expect? I knew open-water swimming was a full-contact sport especially at the outset. It would take awhile for the swimmers to spread out and stop bumping into one another.

I just had to go for it. What an experience! Arms and legs were splashing everywhere. It wasn't until some distance after the second turn buoy I felt like I was far enough away from other athletes that I could get into a rhythm. And "away" is a term I'm using loosely. There were a few times I found myself sandwiched between two guys who seemed as though they were swimming directly toward each other—that is, both of them toward me in the middle. To avoid a collision I had to pop my head up for a brief second to change course and avoid being hit.

The 2.4-mile course was shaped like a large rectangle with three turn buoys, each one marking a turn to the left. From our entry at the pier we would swim parallel to the coastline, then turn left around the first buoy, and swim back in the other direction. Then we'd make a left turn around a second buoy and another left turn around a third, pointing us back toward the pier to complete the course.

My most memorable and spectacular moment in the swim came as I was making my way down the backside of the course. The bottom of the ocean became very desolate, clear and empty—no coral, fish, nothing—just perfect white sand, stretching as far as I could see, like a desert with ripples of sand extending for miles. As I looked below me I spotted a perfectly shaped starfish. My eyes welled up with tears inside my goggles. I was so moved by the perfect reminder of why I was here in Cozumel participating in an Ironman on my mission to raise money for the Foundation's programs to make a difference in the lives of children.

Rebekah had referred to me a month prior as a "starfish thrower"—someone who was giving back, inspiring others, and making a difference, one person at a time. And here I was, racing in the biggest race of my life, standing for a cause I believed in dearly, and I had come upon the most perfectly shaped starfish.

Seeing this one starfish on the sandy bottom as I sped towards the final two buoys, let me know that I had made the right decision and was on the right course, no matter what might be the results of the day's events. Later, on my bike, I wished I had been able to take a photo of that starfish. But it was in that moment I realized, I had! The vision of the starfish is a picture that will forever stick in my mind, engrained as a powerful symbol of what the entire experience meant for me.

As I rounded the last buoy, the sun was in my eyes, making it slightly difficult to see any details of the final stretch to the finish line. However, there were so many swimmers, I just followed the crowd. By that point, I had become more aggressive with swimming and wasn't going to allow the guys to squeeze me out. I held my position, kept stroke and pulled through, propelling myself forward and ahead of them. The water was amazing, making this one of my most peaceful and enjoyable swims. I was out of the water in 1 hour and 17 minutes (quite a bit short of the 2 hours and 20 minutes permitted before the close of the swim course) and thrilled to see such a good time.

## THE BIKE

The walk/run down the dock to the transition area where shower rinse, gear bag, and women's dressing tent were located was actually a long one. I took my time, went to the bathroom, combed my hair and put it in a ponytail, then dried off my feet before putting on my socks and bike shoes. I wanted to embrace the full experience, to be present for every part of it. I walked a long way to get my bike and then wheeled it to the mounting area. I didn't trust myself to run with it, as some were doing.

I stayed calm as I mounted my bike and rode out onto the cobblestones to the Cozumel Highway, heading to the south side of the island on the first of the three loops that made up the 112-mile bike course. There were so many cyclists when I started that I took my time, smiled and thought, *I'm just out for a three-loop ride around the island. No hurry, no race.* My goal was to enjoy the ride and stay present with the experience. After all, this was my first time riding my bike with others, actually participating in a race.

But I picked up the pace on my second loop. I knew I was becoming more comfortable with other riders around me, going through the water stations, and just feeling more comfortable in general. It never struck me that I was probably the only athlete in the entire Ironman who had never been in a bike race of any length before. Attempting an Ironman as a first triathlon, to some, would appear as sheer insanity.

The road along the back side of the island was breezy, subject to the winds coming off the ocean; however, nothing about it frightened me. I smiled and even laughed out loud when a gust of wind shifted my bike. I thought back to what Jack had written in his card: *Hear the wind whispering words of encouragement and support.* I had lots of breezy words of encouragement that day, each one thrilling, never scaring me.

*Me on the windy side of the bike course*

Going through the center of town, which we did on each of the three laps, was a rush. Once I turned left, away from the shore and toward the town, I shifted into a higher gear, and my speed increased to 19-20 mph without any extra effort. For a long-distance racer, having a crowd cheering for you is a welcome "pick me up." I was on the bike for more than six hours, much of it on a two-lane highway closed to all traffic and pedestrians, so no spectators were allowed along the course. The only time a crowd could cheer for me was when I rode through the town.

My last ride through town was tumultuous. Either the wind picked up slightly on my third loop or I just got tired. I don't recall feeling tired, but I do recall the bottoms of my feet hurting and a brief cramp on either my right hamstring or calf. A short panic overcame me, which I countered with a quick mental check-in, telling myself, *It's only a moment. This moment shall pass.* As I repeated those words, I stood up on the bike while pedaling, getting a nice leg stretch to work out the cramp, and was soon good to go.

The dismount area at the end of the third lap was at the City Hall in the center of town. It was such a welcome sight that once, within the dismount chute, I stopped at the very beginning of it instead of riding another 10-15 feet over the timing mat, where my final bike time would be registered. Whoops! I had no idea how this all worked, having never done a triathlon before. It just meant I had to walk a little with my bike before handing it off. My bike computer read 115 miles. Others commented that theirs recorded the same, meaning our course was 3 miles over the expected 112, adding time that no one expected.

## THE RUN

My transition from the bike to the run was again slow. My feet were so sore from the bike pedals, I had to take a few minutes to stretch them. I changed my jersey, ate half a banana and drank an entire bottle of water and most of my electrolyte drink I'd packed in my run gear bag. I even remembered to grab the Jack of Hearts card out of the pouch and placed it in the back pocket of my run jersey. I then hurried back out of the tent to the bathroom and back through again to exit for the run course. Most triathletes don't take the time I was taking and instead wear the same clothes from swim to bike to run, sometimes even relieving themselves while biking and running. This definitely shortens their transition time and thus their overall time; however, it wasn't an approach I was interested in. I wanted to be comfortable and didn't care about shaving off every little minute of time. I was happy to have a good race and finish.

But I will say I certainly wasn't looking forward to running at all, especially 26.2 miles! The run followed the perimeter of the island and consisted of three loops on a paved road. The run course passed many of Cozumel's points of interest, including the waterfront walk, the downtown plaza, and historic neighborhoods. Each loop was tracked as I ran across a timing mat which electronically recorded my time. Race officials monitored each turn to ensure each athlete does not cut the course. This was especially important near the finishing area, where a race official allowed runners on their final lap to make the final turn off the course and toward the finishers' chute.

Once I was on the course, it did not take long for the bottoms of my feet to feel better allowing me to get into a nice running groove. Referencing my running watch, I noted that my first mile was timed at 7 minutes, 40 seconds (7:40), roughly the pace I would keep through mile 6. I remember thinking to myself, *I should slow down because this pace is close to my "stand alone" marathon time*—the time I had run a marathon that was not part of a triathlon. Surely I wouldn't be able to hold it after completing so many hours of swimming and biking. On the other hand, I was running quite comfortably, so I went with it. I eventually slowed to an eight minute pace and then slightly slower by the halfway mark.

Rounding each loop was fun. Crowds of people leaned over the railing with their hands out to slap, a gesture I gladly returned, connecting with several. I'd never done that during a race before. I had always been focused only on keeping my pace. But this time it was different. I let them give me energy and was energized by the exchange.

*Me on the run course*

Heading out for each loop was a mental challenge. I remember telling myself I could walk when I reached two hours. Then I realized I could probably walk the rest of the race and still break 13 hours total, a very respectable time. I had not set a personal goal for finishing, but rather did what I thought I was capable of doing in my mind, staying open and positive. My goal instead was to be present and to enjoy the experience. It was a big deal that I had tackled Ironman before entering any shorter distance triathlons, and so I had chosen not to push myself to set a goal finish time.

Still, I knew that anything could happen in a marathon. I've experienced legs giving out before. *Keep running*, I told myself. It was one mind game after another to stay ahead of the pain and not let it get to me. I replayed the encouraging words that got me through the Boston Marathon; *Pick 'em up and put 'em down,* and Coach Ron's praise that I had more determination than most elite athletes and more strength than most football players. I replayed Ron telling me he would give me his "marathon legs," that I could evoke them in my mind when I needed them. And in my final days of training, I remember Ron saying to imagine my legs feeling light and bouncy like springs, to counter the feeling of muscles filled with lactic acid becoming tight and sore.

Each time I crossed the timing mat, I'd think of my team, friends, and family tracking me. By crossing the mat my information (name, bib number, gender, age category) was remotely viewable via the Internet. I knew I had several people tracking my race electronically, and I certainly didn't want to let any of them down, especially the kids I was raising money to help. I realized on my last loop that if I could keep a 10-minute-per-mile pace, I would break 12 hours and 30 minutes. Wow! Faster than I'd ever imagined! *Keep running!*

By this point my quads, particularly above the knees, were feeling like hardened wooden knots. It was a familiar pain from running marathons, so I knew it was all good and normal. The sun was setting and it was getting cooler –not cool, but cooler. No way was I going to break my stride. In fact, I was passing people. I passed people the entire run. Ron later told me my stats showed I had passed more than 500 people on the run course! I had no idea. I did recall only two or maybe three people passing me.

On this last loop I heard lots of encouraging cheers and many comments about how strong I looked: *Great running! Keep that smile! Look at her go!* And my favorite, *You go, girl! —You know you're kicking butt!* That was my goal, to smile the entire way. When I hurt, I smiled. And the farther into the race I got, I had to go to greater lengths to keep the pain at bay. Each time I took a gulp of Gatorade or water, I imagined the liquid flushing through my aching legs with a cooling relief. I kept thinking, *Okay, Ron, where are your marathon legs?* And I repeated the mantra, *Springy legs, bouncy legs!*

Running that last straightaway, slapping hands with the many spectators, hearing the cheers, passing people, and then rounding the final corner to see the finish line for the first time was incredible. There it was, the grandstands, the ramp up under the official clock, the lights—the finish line! Everything was so loud, but even so, as I crossed the line, I heard the deep voice of the announcer saying very clearly, "Kristy, YOU ARE AN IRONMAN!"

*Crossing the finish line*

I beamed as a volunteer put a finisher medal around my neck. Another volunteer gave me a flower made of sea shells strung on a leather cord. And a third volunteer gave me a hand towel. I thought I'd be gushing tears of joy and anticipated more emotion at the end of such a long, grueling race. I had trained hard and had just finished the longest endurance race of my life, my first triathlon, and had been named an Ironman, a designation so many had told me was impossible. But looking back, I simply was pleased to be done, to have finished. It took a while for reality to set in. Not only had I finished a race against steep odds, but I had finished in a very respectable time. People train for years and years to finish an Ironman and then take longer than I did. I had finished! I had become a triathlete and an Ironman, all in twelve hours and twenty-six minutes (12:26).

*Pinch me, is this real?*

After moving along a pathway to the finishers' photo area and answering simple questions posed by a team of paramedics ("Are you okay?"), I entered the food area, where long tables were set up with different kinds of food and drinks. Walking was a challenge; no cramps, just incredibly tight quads and very achy knees. I didn't dare attempt to sit down, afraid I wouldn't be able to get up again.

I thought I'd be hungry but I couldn't eat more than a few nibbles. My metabolism was going at such a high rate that I had no appetite. It's not uncommon to feel unwell when finishing a race of such length, but I was lucky and didn't have any stomach issues. Later that night I went out with other finishers from Arizona whom I'd met and enjoyed a meal, complete with a bottle of Pacifico.

*Celebrating as I watched others still crossing the finish line*

I wrote in my journal before turning in for bed: *What a day! What a journey! What an experience! I have gone from not owning a bike, to a fear of riding one, to finishing an Ironman in 90 days! Nothing is bigger than me!*

*So, what's next for this Ironman?*

Today, I continue to ask myself this very question, each and every time I reach a milestone. The one thing I do know for certain—*anything is possible.* You can cover great distances by taking just one step at a time. The important part is to take that first step.

## COMING HOME FOR THE GOLF TOURNAMENT

I was on cloud nine. I had just one final goal to complete to meet all four of my 90-day goals. I still had to raise the remainder of the $35,000, and I was not about to fail. Rebekah, the committee, and I had poured everything we had into our golf event. We had sponsors for nearly all 18 holes of the course, we sold the tournament out, and we had collected amazing items for the silent auction.

Having just returned from Cozumel a few days prior, I was still grinning ear to ear. The day felt celebratory and the starting gun had not even sounded. It was heartwarming to see the golf course flooded with people who were there to support my cause and me.

*Stepping off the plane at Phoenix Sky Harbor*

217

The 18-hole tournament finished with a happy-hour reception, silent auction, and short program on my Ironman and The Action Foundation. Just when I thought the day could not get any better, I felt a soft tap on my shoulder. I turned around to see my dad and his wife. They had flown in from Kansas to surprise me just in time to spend the final hours of the reception and celebrate with me. They made it in time to hear the presentation from The Action Foundation and were able to hear about the impact the entire experience had on my life when I shared a few words at the end.

The event could not have run smoother. Everyone had a great time and when the final tally was in, we had raised $36,750!

I had done it. All my goals were met—a picture perfect ending to my 90-day challenge.

## CONNECTING TO A CAUSE

I believe that the people we tend to admire most are the ones who broke through barriers and connected their intention to a cause. They are the ones who connected to something greater than themselves, something that motivated them to move forward each day even when the odds may have felt as though they were stacked against them. The cause became the motivation that drove them through the disappointments.

For me, completing Ironman Cozumel was proof that anything was possible when my intentions were clear. When I dreamt of doing this race it seemed insurmountable. I felt as though the odds were stacked against me, and I constantly felt like I was battling one obstacle or another. It was as though there was a force working against me, trying its best to knock me down. And knock me down it did. I wanted to quit more times than I would like to admit.

I struggled to find rationale to my dream. I struggled to find internal confidence at times. Yet it was having a clear intention and connecting that intention to a cause that served as my motivation. The cause was something far bigger than me that I connected to the goal. What mattered was what the goal stood for and, in turn, what I stood for. The cause was what picked me up every time I was knocked down. It kept me going. It provided me the strength and energy to battle the storm. It was not I alone who succeeded. It was I plus the cause.

Connecting my goal to a cause made everything I did more meaningful. Each experience along the journey served a purpose. It had value and in turn I felt I had a purpose. When times were challenging I found myself stopping and questioning why I was putting myself through such pain. Each and every time I came full circle back to my cause. That was my *why*. My cause wouldn't allow me to quit.

And since quitting was not an option, I had to figure out how to persevere. The only way I knew how to do that was to change my outlook. I had to understand what that particular obstacle was teaching me. As much as I may have tried to fight it, there was always something good that came from every fall. At some point along my journey, each fall became uplifting. I began to cherish each moment so much more. In the end it was the collection of these moments that meant so much more to me than my time on the clock.

## *Play #8: Become Intrinsically Motivated*

Your innate desire to learn, create, and better yourself is what *intrinsically* motivates you. This is your "why" behind any goal. It is your inner desire to direct your own life and improve the world around you. When you are able to connect your goal, to what motivates you intrinsically, you will feel a greater sense of satisfaction.

Having an intrinsic goal and reward also provides for sustainability. You are far more likely to persevere and sustain your efforts than if you chose an external reward such as money. External rewards only provide motivation for a short period. Once your baseline needs are met—for example, you earn enough money—the external reward is no longer worth the effort. But when you are motivated from your deepest values and desires, you keep on going and are capable of greater perseverance in all that you do, becoming unstoppable.

## Kristy's Game Time Coaching
## Journal Entry

What motivates you to fulfill your commitments? What is your "why" behind any task or activity you commit to? What is most important to you about fulfilling them? What does success look like to you? What impact will it have on your life and those around you? The answers to these questions will reveal that the key elements that make you truly unstoppable in everything you do in your life.

# CHAPTER 9

# FINDING AUTHENTICITY: IRONMAN ST. GEORGE AND BEYOND

*People of high self-esteem are not driven to make themselves superior to others. They do not seek to prove their value by measuring themselves against comparative standard. Their joy is being who they are, not in being better than someone else.*
—Nathaniel Branden

Journey to Ironman Cozumel was over and so were my other 90-day program goals that paralleled it. I had been operating at such a fast pace that slowing down felt like coming off an extreme high. But I had actually done it. I had completed all four of my big, hairy, audacious goals and proved to myself that nothing was bigger than me. I was definitely feeling unstoppable.

The exhilaration, and now the slower pace, found me unwittingly returning to a few of my former ways of thinking. My mind turned to the question of what goal I was going to set next. What did I want to accomplish? Did I have another big, hairy, audacious goal to meet?

The downtime after Ironman gave me pause to reflect on other aspects of my life as well. I was less than four months away from my 37th birthday and, with 40 clearly in view, I questioned myself about the direction I was heading. *Where was my life going? Was I living the life I had hoped to be living at this age?*

The hard and honest answer to that last one was no. I had pictured my life at this point to include a family—a loving husband and at least two kids. While I knew I would always maintain my own personal goals and ambitions, I envisioned family to be the core. Unfortunately, I felt this was an area of my life completely outside my control. I could not develop a 90-day plan around my dreams of being happily married and a mom, and that left me feeling emotionally defeated even before I started. The only way I knew how to deal with my emotions was to turn my attention and energy toward results that I could control—or at least had some chance to make happen. But those emotions and my dream to have a family didn't go away.

I had learned the value of vulnerability, of being open and not always in control, when I had to step out of my comfort zone and raise money for the golf tournament. That experience had given me a glimmer of how powerful a result can be when I am open and trusting to bring it about. But I was not yet comfortable with vulnerability in my personal life and sheltered my true personal aspirations from people. I led everyone to believe that the combination of my career, my adventures, and my philanthropic work was fulfilling me. The more I convinced others that I was happy, the easier it became to deny the truth to myself.

I was stuck in this place of deeply wanting something but not knowing how to make it happen. And so, after a month's break from training, I threw myself into my next big goal and set my sights on the next Ironman, just four short months away, with a goal of qualifying for the Ironman World Championship that would take place in Kona, Hawaii.

## SETTING MY SIGHTS ON KONA

My finishing time at Cozumel attracted a lot of positive reactions from other triathletes in my community. Many were impressed, and some amazed. Even those who had filled my head with doubt before the race were genuinely complimentary. I was pleased with my own time, but their reaction gave me a boost in confidence that I could reach for more.

My time was fast under any circumstance, but in my case I'd only had 90 days to train, had never raced a triathlon before, didn't own a bike when I started and didn't hire a coach (I had written my own schedule through research which was confirmed by watching what Jayson was doing). Finishing as I had, in spite of these potential handicaps, had gotten the attention of many in my community. Everyone encouraged me to hire a coach and see how much faster I could get with more structured training. They all thought I could make the cut to enter Ironman Kona, the World Championship, a race that culls the best of the best; it is limited to the top 1,800 finishers from the 28 sanctioned Ironman races a year, making it quite challenging to qualify.

Since I did so well at Cozumel with a fairly uneducated approach, it intrigued me to think what I could do with a coach to direct and track my progress. Also, if there was ever a time to reach for a qualifying time for Kona, the time was now. I might as well build on the physical conditioning and success of my first Ironman. Besides, what else was I going to do? I needed a distraction to keep my mind off the one area in my life that seemed completely outside my reach—my dream of marriage and family.

My search for the best coach in town began. It was purely by being at the right place at the right time, that I met Nick Goodman, owner of Durapulse Performance Company in Scottsdale. Within the first few minutes of talking with Nick, I knew he was the right coach for me. I could tell he would be someone who would push me beyond what I had just achieved on my own, someone I immediately respected and could trust. Of course it did not hurt that he also had faith in me and believed I could make it to Kona.

After much discussion and a few months of training together, we decided on Ironman St. George as my qualifying race. At first, I was totally reluctant to commit to this particular race. Just four months out, there were so many things about St. George I was not excited about. For one, it is held in St. George, Utah, where the swim would be cold and the bike and run courses extremely hilly. In addition, the May 2011 date of the race marked its second year, and it was not yet sold out—both good and bad. It was good from the standpoint that most Ironman races sell out in the first few hours of opening, so if I wanted to qualify for Kona, St. George could be my shot. By the same token, the downside is St. George was only open because the race is touted as the most difficult Ironman in North America, and not everyone rushed to sign up.

The swim portion took place in Sandy Hollow Reservoir, a lake formed by mountain snow runoff, making for frigid, water temperatures. In fact, several of the prior year's contenders told me horror stories of how long they'd sat in the warming tents under blankets before they could feel their extremities enough to get on their bikes.

The bike course after the swim was no picnic either. The course measured nearly 9,000 feet of elevation gain and had one hill referred to as the Wall, which is a mile-long climb at an angle that feels almost completely vertical. Because this was a two-loop course, I would get to climb the Wall twice.

The run course was no friendlier. It had 2,000 feet of elevation gain, comprised of a three-loop out-and-back course, much of which was blocked from spectators. That meant at the end of the race, when my body hurt the most, I'd have to rely solely on my own determination to get me to the finish line. No cheering crowds or shouts of encouragement to goad me on.

Even after completing one Ironman, I still did not love the bike. It was not so much fear of the bike itself that caused my dislike—I had pretty much conquered that fear by Cozumel. It was just that I still had so much to learn. I had never seriously biked hills, I still wasn't using my aero bars (forearms down for maximum aerodynamics) and I absolutely despised traffic. Somehow I had managed to train for Cozumel by avoiding riding on really busy streets. That would not be the case this time now that Nick was coaching me. I would be forced to ride the shoulders of highly trafficked streets in order to get the appropriate hill training. There would be no avoiding it: I still had a great deal of work to do on the bike to get my time where it needed to be in order to finish St. George and qualify for Kona.

## THE FIRST TWO MONTHS

At first I loved every part of my new training, including my coach and teammates—Nick was training a group of nine triathletes at the outset, all aimed at St. George. I even loved the more demanding training schedule. When I started training again, I never thought it would be possible to train longer and harder than when I trained for Cozumel. Still, I loved it. At the time I thought I wanted to do whatever it took to reach Kona.

However, as the first two months of training wore on, I began to question my true intention for doing another Ironman. *Did I really want to qualify for, and conquer, Kona? Or was that someone else's idea of what I should do? Even deeper—Was the training a distraction from what I really wanted in life and didn't know how to get?*

In addition, the reality of training for St. George began to set in. I was only halfway through my training cycle and I was already feeling tired and burned out. If I did qualify for Kona, I would have a month of recovery before starting to train all over again. The three races together—Cozumel, St. George as my qualifying race, and then Kona, the World Championship—meant a year of solid, relentless Ironman training. Any triathlete would agree such a schedule is not recommended, if only from the perspective of sheer burnout. I would definitely be demanding a lot of my body. But it was me, and I was unstoppable, right?

Not yet ready to admit that my interest was waning and my focus was elsewhere, I continued to suppress my true feelings. I had an easy excuse for my declining enthusiasm. I was physically tired from all of the training and my body hurt after nearly every workout. At the same time I continued to tell myself the pain was only natural. Ironman training was supposed to be tough and, in response, the tough get tougher. My attitude made for some very rough training patches those first few months. I shed many tears, made attitude adjustments, and gave myself pep talks. I pressed on.

The Arizona weather in early 2011 did not help matters. We experienced some nights of below freezing temperatures that made for forbiddingly cold early morning workouts at the Phoenix Swim Club, the swim facility Nick encouraged us to train at. One week in particular the forecast predicted 28 degrees at 5:30 a.m., the time when I was scheduled for a Masters class in an outdoor pool. After receiving an email that a local cycling group was canceling their morning ride due to the cold, I sent Nick a text asking if I still had to swim that morning. "Absolutely!" he texted back. "Don't let a little cold water scare you. Think of it as getting into a hot tub."

The next morning I dutifully showed up at the pool precisely at 5:30 a.m., searching for any positive thoughts I could use to help get me in the right frame of mind for my swim workout. I noted that the attendant had pulled back the pool cover of the smaller 25-meter pool instead of the Olympic size 50-meter pool we typically swam in. The pools were heated, of course, and the difference between the air and water temperatures was so great that steam floated along the surface. *A hot tub*, I thought to myself, recalling Nick's words.

Stripping down to a suit in that icy temperature was the tough part. Jumping in the water was actually not as mentally challenging as I imagined—it was so cold on the pool deck, I wanted to be anywhere but there. Thankfully, our Masters swim coach Mark, kept the team moving by instructing us to swim the entire workout in long, individual sets instead of collecting at the wall to wait for the next set to be called out, as in our typical workouts.

Even though the pool was heated, it took longer than usual to warm up, and I'm not so sure my body parts above the water's surface ever got warm. While doing laps, sighting the end of the pool was impossible due to the amount of steam coming off the surface. In fact, there were many times I didn't even realize how close I was to another swimmer until I was right up on their feet and in danger of getting kicked in the face.

Getting out of the pool proved to be the next challenge. The pool deck was frozen over with a thin sheet of ice and my towel and clothes were covered in frost. Strange, but it was just this kind of workout that reminded me of my perseverance and drive, that nothing was bigger than me and I could conquer anything I set my mind to. Having survived the workout, I found myself on a high for the rest of the day.

Training continued to have its ups and downs. Statistically, I was right on target to hit my predicted qualifying time for finishing St. George and earning a spot at Kona. I was making great improvements in all three disciplines: swim, bike, and run. But the qualification process was complicated.

For St. George, it turned out that there would only be two qualifying spots for Kona in my age division, meaning I'd have to come in first or second to qualify. Another race might have more spots to award, based on how many athletes that particular race allows to compete, and then again, how many are competing within the age divisions. It's all percentages. Men's divisions always had more athletes and therefore always got more Kona spots allocated. For Ironman Cozumel and Ironman St. George, I was in Women 35-39, although I was not aiming for a Kona spot in Ironman Cozumel. Unfortunately for me, Women 35-39 was a notoriously tough age group with some of the fastest competitors, while also a division that only awards one to two Kona spots. This is what was lining up for me at St. George; I would be competing in a very competitive spot.

In the world of distance running, where I had done most of my racing, the Boston Marathon was equivalent in stature to Ironman Kona. Like Kona, I had to qualify for Boston by running another marathon under the qualifying time for my age division. It didn't matter if I came in 1st or 31st in my age division, it's the time that counted. I was accustomed to competing against my own time, not necessarily against a group of others for first or second place.

It was a very different mindset to know I'd have to beat out practically all of my competition to win, and so the downs I experienced were mostly mental. I often found myself struggling to find the motivation to complete my workouts, a far cry from my experience training for Cozumel. Instead of pushing through to be an example for The Action Foundation kids, to make a difference, and impact the lives of others in a positive way, I got through my workouts because I had paid a coach to train me, and I couldn't bear to think of myself as someone who quits easily.

## THE NEXT TWO MONTHS

Spring had arrived and the weather was starting to heat up. We had several days break 100 degrees, which brought a new set of physical demands. And the training naturally became more intensive as race day approached.

One Saturday, I had a 120-mile bike ride, all hills, followed by a 9-mile run, again all hills. The temperature reached about 100 degrees. When it was all said and done, I was out on the road for nine hours straight. Most of my time I spent alone, having been left in the dust by my faster male teammates in the early miles. Guys are naturally stronger on the bike due to their leg muscles, and the guys on my team were all experienced triathletes. That day I got up before 5:00 a.m. to be on my bike by 6:00 a.m., and I did not complete my run until after 3:00 p.m.

The bike ride was tough. In addition to the hilly terrain, the wind was blowing hard and constantly changed directions. It felt as though I was constantly fighting a headwind no matter what direction I rode. At mile 83 my legs were fatigued, and I began to suffer the effects of a dehydration headache even though I had gone through many water bottles, one after another. At one point riding up a hill into a headwind, while pushing as hard as I could, I looked down at my bike computer to see I had slowed to 12 mph. It was just too much for me, and I began to cry (yes, it is possible to cry while riding a bike). But before long, my disappointment turned to anger, which fueled another round of energy. Shortly thereafter, I sped up to 20 mph up the hill, still into the wind.

I'd like to say it ended there but I had an equally miserable run. Finally off the bike with my legs hurting, I was hungry and tired, and I so badly wanted to just be done. I was still alone and only by an act of pure will was I able to lace my shoes. Not long into the run I reached what I referred to as San Francisco Hill, named after the steeply graded streets of that city. This hill is so steep at a 16% grade it had earned a caution sign for vehicles. My legs told me to walk the hill, yet my mind focused on running, regardless of how slow or painful it might become. I was also dehydrated; I ran out of water 30 minutes into the run and never saw a place to refill my bottle until the last mile before reaching my car. I was so thirsty that I nearly flagged down a passing vehicle to see if they had any water I could drink. Pure determination got me through the run.

I thought I had failed my workout that day. However, Nick showed me that statistically I was still making improvements and was on track to reach my qualifying time. I couldn't give up now. I had too much invested to even consider it.

As the race day grew closer, I did everything I was told to do. I visualized my race-day performance, I increased my sleep, and I never cut a workout short. Still, there was something missing. It was not physical. My body was ready and in better cardio shape than it had been for Ironman Cozumel. It was not mental. I had no major fear of the bike or the hills I had to climb, and I knew I could survive the cold of the water, even if it was not going to be fun.

*So what else was there?*

Slowly, I allowed myself to acknowledge what had been there for quite some time. I had lost my passion, my clear intention, my *why*, the backbone of the commitment I had made to myself since the summit of Mt. Kilimanjaro. Coming down that mountain in 2009, I'd promised myself that everything I did in life going forward would serve a purpose, a greater good. Everything I would do in life would make a difference to someone or something.

*So why was I doing this race?* My efforts fit neither of those parameters.

I had been clear about my goal to qualify for Kona, the World Championship. But I had to ask myself, *Am I clear on my bigger intention? Was Kona my own vision or had others put that vision into my mind by telling me I could achieve it? What impact did racing Kona even make? Did it better someone's life? Did it better my life?* This kind of internal querying grew more and more intense, keeping me up at night and sapping me of motivation and enthusiasm. Yet, I continued to train.

I knew Kona would be an amazing experience, a memory of a lifetime, and something I could check off my bucket list. But at this point in my life, after everything I had learned about the value of having a purpose and standing for a cause, checking something off a list didn't really seem all that important anymore.

The other side of my brain assessed the situation and decided I was not a quitter. I was not the type to let myself off the hook just because things got tough. In fact, the tougher things got, the more driven I became. And by this point I'd invested too much time and energy, and was too close to the actual event, to give it all up. With all that rationalization going through my mind, I still could not shake the fact I truly wanted to quit this time. Regardless of these thoughts, I soldiered on.

## BECOMING AUTHENTIC

Every day it became clearer that the pure physical challenge was no longer enough for me. Adding Ironman Kona to my resume was no longer motivating. I was missing the resolve I brought down the mountain to make my life about something more than myself. Just having a goal and clear intentions was not everything. Connecting the intention to a cause that I was passionate about is what kept me going on Kili and at Cozumel.

I was not authentically experiencing my own personal fulfillment. I recalled what Ron, my 90-day program coach, had said in parting, "It's great that you do all of these things for others. But what are you doing to create your own future? When are you going to take the same energy and put it towards your own fulfillment?"

I truly did not understand the value of his inquiry at the time. I was on a high from meeting all of my goals, including an after-school fitness program I had just funded for 200 kids the coming year. Yet months later, struggling to meet this new goal, all the pieces started to come together.

Giving to others seemed to be organically engrained in my heart. It was always there for me in the background of everything I did and, when missing, it stood out like a sore thumb. But at the same time, while it was great to be outwardly focused, to think of others and contribute to worthy causes I cared about, I needed to also take care of myself—to give myself what I authentically wanted. And I hadn't been doing that.

Ron's comment was not about treating myself to pedicures, fancy dinners out, or a new outfit. He was talking about the importance of me focusing my attention on myself to ensure that I would experience my own personal fulfillment. Simply stated, this meant being authentic with my desires and living my life with clear intentions, not just outward goals or goals that benefitted others. For me, contributing to the lives of others is an important part of who I am. I realized through my training that my ability to give to others required first that I was personally fulfilled. It was through my own fulfillment that I had the energy to give to others.

The next question then seemed obvious. *Where in my life was I unfulfilled? Where was I lacking abundance? What was it that I truly wanted that I did not yet have?*

I finally allowed myself to admit it. All I wanted, I realized, after all of my accomplishments in career and sports, was to be part of a loving family, to become a wife and mother and give my family all of the riches I had stored up over my lifetime of experiences. It was the area of my life I felt helpless to impact and emotionally stopped by, yet it remained my priority, conscious or unconscious, and it would not go away.

I will never forget the Saturday bike ride that followed my revelation. I often biked in Fountain Hills, a town just east of where I lived. I chose to do my long rides there because, as the name implies, the town is hilly. It was also far enough away from both Scottsdale and Phoenix that there was significantly less traffic.

Long training rides often equated to spending an entire day on the bike. On this particular ride, I was at the halfway mark around mile 50 when I stopped at the town park to refill my water bottles. The park was filled with young kids climbing on the jungle gym, while others were throwing balls with their parents. A few families were enjoying picnics on the green grass overlooking the lake and fountain. As I drank I watched the happy scene and felt a heavy tug at my heart. As I got back on my bike, sadness filled my heart. And as I rode away, I knew that I no longer wanted to spend my days on a bike. I wanted to create my future, a future with a partner—Saturdays with a husband and kids, picnicking at the park.

That Saturday was like so many of my Saturdays spent training for Ironman St. George: alone and struggling with waning motivation. I had plenty of time to wonder and think. I knew what I really wanted, but how was it ever going to happen for me?

I knew it would happen at some point, but there wasn't much I felt I could do to control the timing. My faith told me that God would provide the perfect partner when He saw fit. The hardest part of faith is letting go and realizing things may not always happen when I think I am ready for them. Important things in life happen on their own time. Nevertheless, I had difficultly preventing these longings and desires from influencing my already flagging motivation in training for the next Ironman.

## Letting Love In

My growing longing to be part of something, a family of my own, paralleled certain events in my personal life. For many months leading up to my current training cycle I had avoided dating. In fact, I made it a point not to accept any dates during my 90-day challenge and I expected that trend to continue. I wanted to spend time singularly focused on my goals and allow for any self-discovery to unfold as it may. Dating would be a distraction, taking my focus off my training and self-discovery and placing it on someone else.

I had also come to the point in my life where dating was not something I enjoyed. I had been married once and had learned much from that experience. The second time around, I felt I knew what qualities I wanted in a mate and had no interest in taking the time to explore any type of relationship with someone outside the perfect fit. In fact, I often joked that I would rather spend an evening home with Kingston, my dog, than out with someone not fitting my vision of the future.

When I hired Nick and committed to my St. George training with the goal of qualifying for Kona, my work and my training had once again become my life. But the feeling that something was missing kept coming up as I progressed, and I was forced to look more authentically at my life. It's true that this self-reflection caused a chink in my armor, a crack in the door that had been firmly closed. Perhaps this is why two months into my training, I accepted an invitation from an old friend to attend a charitable gala. Little did I realize that this event would mark the beginning of a new relationship.

I had met Tim nearly a decade earlier when we both joined a running group and hired a coach to help us reach our marathon goals. The group became close and would frequently travel together for regional road races. Tim and I kept in touch over the years that followed but not with any real consistency. Sure we had mutual friends and naturally heard about each other's endeavors but more from a distance. Our paths crossed occasionally, both socially and professionally, yet never led to any kind of constant communication.

In 2009 we connected when we were both named to the Phoenix Business Journal's *Forty Under 40* list, acknowledging rising young professionals. Then, in 2010, working on his own bucket list, Tim drove his Jeep solo from Arizona to the Arctic Circle and back. He contacted me to see if he could borrow any cold weather gear I had on hand from my climb up Mt. Kilimanjaro. The call turned into lunch, a hike, and a couple of dinners. In late 2010 Tim tracked my progress throughout my 90-day program and even donated to my cause.

In February 2011 I received an email from Tim announcing his new marathon goal, but it also included an invitation. He needed a date for a gala being held by the Catholic Community Foundation. This gala, with its focus on charitable giving, was considered the premier Catholic social event in the Valley and would be attended by more than 700 people. Tim was attending because he was on the board of a local bank, and the bank's president, as this year's gala chairperson, had purchased a table to fill with several board members. In addition, Tim's older brother Michael was to be the keynote speaker.

The gala, Tim wrote, was to be held the first weekend in March. Thinking this was clearly a business proposition, I easily accepted. The next three weeks were filled with sporadic, random, and fun emails between us, catching up on past times and sharing a few good jokes.

On the Sunday prior to the gala the tone of our upcoming venture noticeably changed. Tim called on the phone instead of e-mailing.

"I thought we should actually talk, even have dinner, before our first date," he said on the phone.

"What? A date?" I asked. "I thought this was a business arrangement."

"It is," he assured me. "But I'm also interested in dating you, maybe pursuing a relationship," he said, his voice confident yet casual. After a pause, he said, "And I have been for quite some time." Apparently, I'm not the most approachable person to ask out, given the tenacious focus I'd had toward my goals, and Tim had been waiting for just this opening.

Extremely flattered, I accepted his invitation to have dinner the night before the gala. But as the days counted down I found myself becoming nervous. *What if I don't see him the same way he sees me?* We had known each other for so long and, as much as I liked him, I had never considered dating him. In some vague way I must have decided he was just not my type.

But the crack in the door was widening, and I found myself reconsidering what I thought was true. Interestingly, just hours before Tim called that Sunday night to announce his true intentions, I had enjoyed tea and conversation with two girlfriends. During our discussion about our personal lives, I realized just how narrow-minded I'd been all these years. Not so long before, I'd made a list of things I wanted in a life partner. Thinking back to that list, I realized it was actually a description of myself. All these years I had been looking to date me—or someone just like me. I saw how that kind of relationship would have lacked dimension and richness, and maybe wasn't ideal.

My insight led to a new realization. I asked myself, *If I don't necessarily want a partner who was exactly like me, then what kind of partner do I want?* The answer came quickly and simply: I just want to find someone who is happy. I wanted someone who lived his life with no regrets, having sought after and accomplished his personal goals and was at peace within himself on that account—as was I. If we were both happy and fulfilled in all that we had been doing in life, then it made sense that us sharing that abundance would make us happy with each other.

Coming to this new revelation, I could not help but think about men in my life that I might have missed or overlooked in the past. As I drove home from that tea and conversation with my girlfriends, it was actually Tim who first came to mind. Perhaps it was because we had exchanged emails for the last three weeks and had this gala coming up; nevertheless, I had always enjoyed my time with him. Our connection was always natural, comfortable, and just plain fun. And approaching 40, he had spent plenty of good quality time alone, most recently on his Arctic Circle trip, finding himself. It was clear to me that Tim had found his own internal happiness and was living authentically in accordance with his heart and his goals.

Looking back on my training struggles for St. George, I was already questioning my own intentions regarding my goal in the first two months, prior to my first date with Tim. However, my questioning took new shape in the months that followed. Having Tim in my life showed me that there was more to life than work and training, and I found myself wanting to share more of my life with him.

Tim was an incredible support. When I questioned my goal, he reminded me that I was not a quitter. I am strong, I am tough, and I am determined. He always liked to remind me that I would be a two-time Ironman after St. George. I will admit I did like the sound of that. I knew I would be proud of my accomplishment even if I did not qualify for Kona. Even more, I knew I would be proud to share the experience with my future children.

What followed, was the beginning of our relationship. I think it was a combination of our age, life experiences, personal successes, internal happiness, and the almost decade of knowing each other that provided the right situation for our relationship to flourish fairly quickly.

By the time Ironman came along, we had been together two months. We did not discuss the topic of getting married or having kids much, which was what I had identified as the missing component in my life. We were still enjoying the newness of our relationship and getting to know each other at a deeper, more intimate level. And I liked the stage we were in. We were still learning how the other person processed information and made decisions and, along with that, the best ways to communicate with each other.

Yet at a very deep, subconscious level, I slowly began to trust in him more, releasing some of my need to control and becoming more vulnerable on a personal level. Parallel to that inner development, I was seeing clearly what it was that I wanted in life, and I felt myself naturally being drawn into the authentic life I had been wanting all along.

## RACE DAY — IRONMAN ST. GEORGE

May 2011 finally arrived. I had survived my training and now it was time to see what I could do over the 140.6-mile course on race day. Tim and I loaded up my bike in his Jeep and made the 432-mile drive from Phoenix to St. George, Utah. After arriving, we spent a day and a half handling registration, packing my transition bags, and checking them into the appropriate locations. Along the drive to St. George, we drove part of the 112-mile bike route and the 26.2-mile run course so Tim could get a lay of the land and better understand the road closures on race day. I was grateful he wanted to be positioned along the course, and we found a spot to maximize the number of times he would see me. I will never forget his impression of the run course. He thought it was the hilliest marathon route he had ever seen and that it was pretty outrageous to stick it in an Ironman.

I know I was not exactly the easiest person to be around those last few days leading up to the race. I was still dealing with the tremendous conflict regarding my motivation constantly running through my mind. I struggled with if merely finishing this race was enough. Yet I also knew if I did qualify for Kona, I would be put in a position I knew I did not want to face. If I qualified and accepted the position,

I would have one month off before I had to start training for my third Ironman. I knew I did not want to do that. Yet I also knew if I qualified, I would not be able to turn down the spot. There was no winning solution. I tried my hardest to turn my energy toward doing my best and letting that be enough.

Like Cozumel, I was calm and focused on race morning. In the blackness of the early morning hours, I arrived at the lake with my teammates in plenty of time to top off my tires, visit the port-a-potty, and get into my wetsuit. Just as the sun was coming up, we entered the water as a team. With hundreds of people in the water, I quickly lost track of my teammates. We entered well ahead of the gun time, perhaps a little too early for my liking. The water was cold, and treading only seemed to churn up the cooler water along the lake bottom making me that much colder.

Finally, the gun went off. I swam the 2.4 miles nonstop. I remained very cold and toward the end I counted down the time until I reached the shore. Once out of the water, I quickly glanced at the clock to discover my swim time was slower than I had expected, what we calculated was necessary for me to stay within the top placements in my age division. Despite being a faster swimmer after months of intense training, my time was slower than my Cozumel time. I had to push any thoughts surrounding my slower time out of my mind and keep moving. I still had a long day ahead of me.

I tried running to pick up my transition bag for the bike but could not move faster than a slow walk. My feet were cold and stiff from the water. With each step I felt a tingling yet painful sensation. Once inside the changing tent, I had a volunteer help me into my socks and cycling shoes. It was a good thing since I could not feel if my socks were even on smoothly. After getting my socks on I remember the volunteer trying to massage my feet, thinking it would warm them up, but I quickly pulled my feet back as the pressure from the massage only made them feel worse.

After getting my cycling shoes on, my feet turned numb. I was unable to feel my foot placement and my plan to run to my bike turned into a painful walk. I took even more time getting my bike off the rack and wheeling it into the mounting area. I laughed at myself as I seemed to take forever to get clipped into the pedals. Tim told me later that I actually clipped in easily. My feet were just so numb from the cold water that I could not feel that they were attached to the pedals.

Like Cozumel, my routine in training was to eat half of a peanut butter and honey sandwich halfway through my ride. I learned my stomach needed a break from the gels and welcomed solid food at that point. Just a few feet after I left the mounting area, I heard something drop. Was that my sandwich? Sure enough, my sandwich had fallen out of my jersey pocket. Already behind in my projected time and not wanting to create a hazard for the other riders, I didn't stop and get off my bike to pick it up. With a deep breath, I told myself, *It's ok. You still have solid food in your special needs bike bag.* This was one of the bags I packed the day before to be placed around mile 52 on the bike course with items I might need, such as a spare tire and extra nutrition.

I rode my first loop with ease. While rounding the corner to begin my second loop, I rode through a crowd comprised of Tim and my other teammates' spouses which gave me a little extra boost. I was entering the backside of the mountain where all the climbing takes place and I would be completely isolated from spectators. I needed to carry that energy with me for the next 48 miles, including my second trip up the Wall, the hardest climb on the bike route.

It was a beautiful day, warmer than expected and completely sunny with not a cloud in the sky. While that kind of weather makes for a beautiful spectator day, it is not exactly ideal for the athletes. The heat and the sun cause the athletes to sweat more, depleting their bodies of electrolytes. For that reason, it was important to hydrate with not only water but also an electrolyte-packed energy drink, like Gatorade, to replace the sodium and other minerals that the body sweats out. Race organizers supply both water and electrolyte drinks along the course.

Having already lost my sandwich in the mounting area, I had nothing solid to eat and would have to rely on the food packed in my special needs bag to fuel me. As I approached mile 52 and the area where special needs bags were available, I listened closely to hear my race number called and looked for the volunteer holding it out as I rode by, which would allow me to grab it without stopping. But unfortunately, the volunteer responsible hadn't pulled my bag out in time, and I never heard my number. Seconds after I passed he realized I'd already gone by and came running after me, yelling my number and holding my bag. But it was too late. I would have had to stop, get off my bike, and either turn around or wait for him to run up to me. At this point I was reminded of my coaching: *every minute counts*. So I shook my head no and kept riding. This would turn into a major strategic mistake.

I had only gels, water, and electrolyte drink left to provide fuel. It was not the nutrition plan I had trained with or planned for race day, yet it was the hand I was dealt. As I rounded the backside of my second loop I began to feel the effects of not having any solid food. My stomach began to cramp. It was much too early. I still had more than 40 miles to ride and a 26.2-mile run to complete.

I decided to take the extra time to stop at the next water station, get off my bike, and use the port-a-potty. Perhaps that would give me some relief. But there was a line waiting and it did not make for a quick stop. At Cozumel I never stopped once. And I knew now that racing for a Kona spot meant I had to be mindful of every minute. I also knew that my competition, those Kona bound hopefuls, had the same mindset. Many of them would resort to relieving themselves on the bike while riding, their urine running down their seat, bike, and leg. This was something I could not bring myself to do, even for a Kona spot.

I continued to stay positive, still feeling strong on the bike, and when I finished I was proud of how I rode. In the dismount area, still with an upset stomach, I chose not to run through the transition area, but rather walked. Much to my surprise, even with all of the water and electrolyte drink I consumed, I did not need to use the port-a-potty again, I changed into my running shoes and off I went, starting the run course with the best smile I could muster. But it wouldn't take long before my smile was no longer able to convince my body it felt good. I began taking frequent visits to the port-a-potty to vomit. No longer able to stomach any gels, I handed them over to Tim as soon as I saw him along the course. Before I knew it, I was walking the aid stations, praying my stomach would settle enough to run or, at the very least, shuffle my feet. With each visit to a port-a-potty, I thought for certain my vomiting would empty out the cramps. But relief never seemed to come.

On the second loop of the run I saw another competitor I recognized from Arizona walking in pain. No longer caring about my time, I joined him. This was when a huge part of me gave up. I allowed myself to give into the physical discomfort. Because I had him by my side, I walked far longer than I care to admit. Still in and out of port-a-potties, walking did not seem to provide relief to my cramping stomach.

A few days prior Tim and I had driven the run course and noticed the huge floodlights that were set along the course. Tim explained that these would come on after the sun set for those still running. Athletes had until midnight, a full 17 hours, to complete the course and still be called an Ironman. Now on my final loop, I noticed the sun was beginning to set behind the mountain and I remembered Tim's words, *You are not going to need those lights.* Seeing them and recalling what he'd said was my trigger to pick up my pace. Despite my stomach, I started to jog. I had lost focus in my race and, as a result, lost sight of my finishing time. But now I just wanted to beat the floodlights.

Regardless of my newfound drive, I still had brief moments of walking to try and compose myself. I no longer allowed myself to walk for long and kept myself going by repeating to myself, *Pick 'em up and put 'em down.* Finally, I crossed the finish line in 13 hours and 52 minutes, much slower than my goal of 11 hours and 50 minutes. Not at all proud of myself, I managed a smile and raised my hands over my head as I crossed the finish line. At least I was done!

Walking through the finisher's area, I didn't feel the pain in my legs as I had at Cozumel. I knew this was because I had not given it my all. Tim, coach Nick, and several of my teammates met me in the finisher's area and sat with me while

I did my best to get some food down. Still nauseated and realizing my chemistry was completely off, I forced myself to suck the salt off a few French fries and pickles. It was about all I could manage at the time, and it did help.

Celebrating that night was not at all like I had envisioned. Instead of dinner out with a beer, I spent the night on the bathroom floor, hardly sleeping and with not a lot in my stomach. Thankfully by sunrise things felt more promising— at least for me. Tim had gotten a terrible sunburn on his legs while watching the race and by the morning was limping on swollen shins as he wheeled my bike from our hotel room to the Jeep for the trip back home. I, on the other hand, jogged back into the hotel dining room to snag a couple of cookies for the road. To any observer, it would have appeared that he had competed the day before, and I was the one there for support!

To put a cap on the whole experience, I did not reach my initial goal of qualifying for Ironman Kona. The St. George Ironman 2011 had allotted only two qualifying spots into Kona for my age group and the two fastest women accepted. That year there were two very fast women in my age group. It was at least comforting to know that even if I did have the perfect race and met my projected finishing time, I would not have qualified. Still to this day Ironman St. George remains at the top of the list for "Toughest Ironman Courses," as rated by the website RunTri.com. In 2011 more than 1,600 athletes started but only 1,311 finished the race, all with slower times compared to other courses. This meant more than 300 athletes did not finish this race, giving it a 19% DNF (did not finish) rate, the highest of any Ironman course. In 2013 Ironman St. George was shortened to a Half Ironman, 70.3 miles, in hopes of encouraging participation.

## THE AFTERMATH

I spent the weeks and months that followed analyzing my race. What had happened? In spite of the tough course, I was in better physical shape than I had been for Ironman Cozumel. I had the confidence of having gone the distance at Cozumel, and I had trained on the St. George course before the race multiple times. I swam, biked, and ran the paces I needed to meet my goal time, and I visualized winning my race. I did everything I could and still came up short of my projected finishing time.

Certainly I could use the excuse I had stomach issues. But in reality, so what if I'd been in pain? An Ironman is painful. In fact, any endurance sport is going to bring a level of pain. Endurance comes down to being mentally tough, pushing through adversity and all physical barriers. The human body is an amazing machine. It can and will adapt to any situation. And the human mind is a powerhouse. It is this powerhouse that enables a person to push far beyond the physical limits the body may feel possible.

I remember the specific run I was on one warm Saturday morning in August of 2011, three months after St. George, when I had my "aha" moment. I was training for my next marathon, one that Tim had signed us both up for which, ironically, was to be held in St. George, Utah. It was on this run that all of my experiences finally tied together. I suddenly knew why I had endured the disappointments I had, as well as experienced the sense of soaring to new heights with some of my accomplishments. Thinking back to that day, it took me feeling pretty low, as though I was at the bottom of a well looking up toward a glimmer of light, to understand the bigger picture.

It was this Saturday morning when I had to drag myself to the base of Mummy Mountain for a 16-mile hill training run, in the heat, before sunrise, solo. I was not feeling particularly good about myself that day. In fact, I was feeling downright deflated. I was still beating myself up about my race day performance at the St. George Ironman. I was depressed about the weight I had gained since the race and still not taken off, I was not motivated by my professional life, and, to top it off, I was winded and out of breath by only mile six.

It did not take long before I became cranky about the heat and the fact that I ran out of water with no water fountain in sight. This only reminded me how much I despised Arizona's scorching hot summers. I had always planned to make enough out of my career that I could afford a summer house in San Diego. Well, truth be told, I really wanted to raise my kids with summers in San Diego. Oh yeah, perhaps I should remind myself I was 37 and still not married. *Kids? What was I thinking? Were none of my personal life's dreams ever going to come true?* It was one of those days where nothing seemed to be stacked in my favor, or so I thought.

It was on this particular run I pondered why it was that I wasted all that time training for a second Ironman, only to perform below my ability and be left feeling worse than when I started. *Why had I not stopped after the first Ironman and just basked in my glory?*

Always believing that everything happens for a reason, I still failed to understand the reason behind the months of agony I had just put myself through. It was this dreadful mile six when I felt my walls begin to crumble. Hot and parched, I considered chancing the risk of drinking contaminated water from someone's sprinkler system just to quench my thirst. It was then my eyes filled with tears. I cannot recall thinking about anything in particular at this point. I just felt empty.

And then it happened. I suddenly had clarity. It was as though someone flipped on the light switch in the room. Instantly, I smiled, felt chills cover my body, and began to cry. Only they were tears of happiness. I finally understood. I knew why I needed to push through to the end of that race, despite knowing deep in my heart I no longer wanted to train. I no longer wanted to achieve what I originally set as my goal.

I had not really failed at all. My success was just wrapped in a different package than I originally envisioned. Success did not come in the form of a Kona qualifying spot. It came wrapped with a much different bow. And it took me three months to pull the tie to see what was hidden inside. At that moment I knew I was exactly where I was supposed to be at that point in my life, at that very moment. I was once again present.

For the past three months I had lugged the weight of failure on my back. As heavy as I allowed it to get and as miserable as I allowed it to make me feel, I was now grateful for that ordeal. Had I not carried that weight long enough for it to get heavy, I never would have forced myself beyond the belief that I get everything I ever wanted in life on my own terms, on my watch, just because I have the ability to persevere. Had this belief become so entrenched in my mind that I didn't take anything away from all of my past experience? Am I incapable of applying what I learned universally in my life? If I want to grow, I must be open to new experience, embrace the outcomes, good or bad, and allow them to transform me.

It was through Alcatraz I learned the power of my mind. My experience on the Pole taught me to adapt to change, applying knowledge from my past experience but also yielding to the present moment in trusting my instincts, not just my physical ability alone. Through climbing Kilimanjaro and Journey to Ironman Cozumel, I discovered the power of finding what I was passionate about and connecting to a cause to motivate me through the tough times. Yet it was the weight of my Ironman St. George failure that showed me the bigger lesson: Without being true to myself and ensuring my deepest personal needs are fulfilled, then the combination of living with a purpose, the power of my mind, and the motivation of a cause is just plain not enough. None of that alone would ever lead me to real fulfillment or happiness.

It was through the agonizing months of training for St. George, pushing myself to reach for a goal I knew in my heart I no longer wanted, the goal of Ironman Kona, for me to break down and see my bigger purpose in life. Prior to those months of struggles, only pieces of my purpose had been uncovered. Or at least I was not yet willing to admit the rest. I was very much in tune with my professional purpose; it was my personal purpose that I continued to suppress. Keeping my focus on the task at hand, still trying to convince myself that I wanted Kona, I turned to the power of my mind to distract me from what I was too afraid to face: my personal life.

I had proven so many times before that I could push through anything. And this time, in terms of Ironman, I was even better prepared physically. Yet race day had a different agenda in mind. Struggling through my stomach issues and underperforming taught me that the power of the mind is not enough. Having a clear intention is not enough. I had denied myself one piece, perhaps the most important piece—taking care of myself and seeing that I was living authentically to my deepest desires and values.

I am not just referring to eating well, exercising, and getting enough sleep. I realized that taking care of myself went much deeper. It was about being true to myself, being authentic, and acting with courage. It meant allowing myself to be vulnerable enough to take risks and go after the things in life I truly wanted, and letting go of control—the things that would require an investment that had no certain guarantee.

My entire life I had known I wanted to be a wife and a mother. Yet for the last 37 years, I denied admitting to anyone the importance of marriage and motherhood in my life. In fact, most of the time I even denied admitting it to myself. I grew up surrounded by professional success. In my eyes success was independence and looked like a suit and a briefcase, not a dependent, stay-at-home mom. My professional life and the accolades I received for excelling had fulfilled me, and I was proud of my achievements.

While on paper my accomplishments were impressive, I continued to strive for more. At first, it was just extra curricular activities. Then it evolved into my search for something, a piece of me that seemed unfulfilled, missing, unsatisfied. Embarking on new adventures and challenging myself to reach new levels would appease my senses in the moment. Apparently, they also filled a void I had not yet identified. As soon as one challenge was done, I quickly turned my attention to something new. Nothing was ever enough, and there was never a dull moment.

While these adventures may have served as my form of avoidance, my way of suppressing my feelings and building a distraction from the things in life I wanted most, they were also my way of exploration. Regardless of the reason, it was through these final years of physical challenges that I gained clarity on my purpose in life. It actually took the feeling of failure, experiencing disappointment and surviving heartbreaks that proved to me I am strong, resilient, and courageous. I am worthy of complete happiness and living out all of my dreams. And the only way I am going to fully realize them is through being true to myself.

It was time for me to face the truth of what was missing from my life. It was a piece that would put me in the most vulnerable position yet; something that required dependence on a partner, a risk I would have to invest in with no guarantee. Yet I could no longer deny what my heart desired. I wanted nothing more than to be a wife and a mother. And if it meant giving up a career that I had worked so hard for and the crazy adventures I seemed to live for, I was willing to do it.

## MY AUTHENTICITY

I learned that my greatest purpose in life was to combine my passion, professionally and personally, to make a difference in all I do. My cause is to empower others to reach their full potential by supporting them to create the change they desire in their lives. I also want to take care of and raise a family to continue a legacy of giving in ways that is unique to my children's personalities.

Acknowledgement became power. There was power in writing down my purpose, both professionally and personally. There it was in black and white, my truth. There was no way to deny it. Throughout the next several months, even year, I spent time looking at the things that were standing in my way of reaching my truth. *Were my actions in alignment? Was I focusing my time and energy on the things that would get me to my truth?*

For the most part, I would say yes professionally. It was the personal side I needed to refocus. I was developing a relationship with Tim, and I naturally felt the desire to shift more of my attention to spending time with him. The decision felt easy. I was having fun and we were creating such amazing experiences together. The hardest part about this investment for me was becoming vulnerable. I was investing in someone else, someone with ambition, dreams, and opinions rather than the investments I was accustomed to making in things— things I ultimately had control over.

Two things happened in our time together. First, I applied the lessons I learned from my adventures into my state of being. I looked at how I was showing up rather than the results I was creating. In a relationship with others, there is no control over the results. Yet if you stay true to yourself, your being, you will attract the same. And secondly, it didn't hurt that Tim was the first to call me out when I was placing control in our relationship. While I must be driven to hold myself accountable, it is important to surround myself with support. And Tim was just that for me.

Fourteen months later, in October 2012, Tim surprised me with a proposal. We were in Cabo San Lucas, Mexico, alone on a rooftop patio overlooking the water at sunset. Complete with a soft breeze and a gorgeously lit-up sky, it was the perfect moment. "Do you want to get married?" he said. But I was so shocked, I returned his question with a question—three times! I didn't know whether he wanted to have a discussion about getting married or if he was actually proposing—a yes or no question. Still to this day, we get a good laugh recalling that moment.

We were married three and half months later on Tim's parents' property. The ceremony was simple and perfect in every way. Surrounded by the love and support of our immediate family, we stood in the front yard in the shadow of the head of Camelback Mountain, a predominant peak in Phoenix, and were married at sunset. Cocktails and a four-course dinner followed the ceremony. We enjoyed our meal on a covered patio at a candlelit table set for 19; a fireplace crackled in the background and sheer white curtains enclosed us, shielding us from the cool desert night. The evening was filled with fun and laughter, which is exactly how we envisioned our lives together.

Five months later, I learned of a program called Sports Life Coaching that pulled together everything I wanted to do professionally into one career. Through this program I would learn to be a life coach using sports terminology to help empower others to live authentically, creating the results in their life they desire. This perfectly combined my purpose to help others with my love for sports. This also gave me the opportunity to set up my own business, allowing Tim and me the flexibility to raise our future children the way we envisioned. Two months later I left my career of 17 years for this new adventure.

I had learned that becoming unstoppable was much more than perseverance, presence, and adaptability. At the very foundation is authenticity, which requires constant work and self-awareness in knowing my truth. Being unstoppable is not a plateau I reach and then coast along for eternity. It is more like a continuously revolving door with one hallway leading to the next. When I step out of the door, there is always another challenge waiting for me on the other side. There will also be times I feel as though I am stuck in that door, going around and around in circles with no way out. I now know to accept and embrace these times, and have confidence that it is in these endlessly repeating revolutions that I become more resilient.

Looking back over the past six years, I could see that it was through so many triumphs and frustrations that I gained the clarity to know what I truly wanted. I found my own authenticity—and so can you.

## Play #9: Create Personal Fulfillment

Finding your authenticity is like finding your core. It is an expression of your essential self, uncensored and unimpeded by external forces. It takes courage to find what makes you uniquely you, rather than what you believe you should be based on social pressures. Living authentically means living true to your personality, spirit, and character.

When you live authentically, you create personal fulfillment. You are living intentionally toward a purpose rather than completing a task simply to check it off the list. It can make all the difference in a satisfying life—you deserve it!

# Kristy's Game Time Coaching
# Journal Entry

Create your Legacy Statement. Whatever fulfills you personally is your legacy—all that you leave behind when all is said and done and your life has meant something that mattered to you and others.

What do you want your life to stand for? In one to two sentences, summarize what you want people to remember about you. What legacy do you want to leave behind? From this moment forward, measure your actions against your statement. Are you living on purpose? With intent? Are you personally fulfilled?

# EPILOGUE

## *AN INSURMOUNTABLE OBSTACLE SURMOUNTED*

*As you become more clear about who you really are,
you'll be better able to decide what is best for you—
the first time around.*
—Oprah

On December 6, 2013 my world changed, at least the world according to my dreams. It was the day I was told that my husband and I had less than a 5% chance of conceiving a child, even with the help of the most advanced fertility medicine available.

While sitting across the table from the top fertility specialist in Arizona, I did my best to keep my composure. I had come in for a 15-minute test, expecting the results to be given the following week when Tim would accompany me. However, because the doctor felt it necessary to discuss what he'd found in the test, I was alone receiving the news that dramatically impacted us both.

I tried to stay present by focusing on my doctor's every word, hoping to prevent my mind from jumping too far ahead. My diagnosis was *premature ovarian failure,* a condition that happens when a woman's ovaries stop functioning before the age of 40. When the ovaries fail they no longer release eggs regularly and infertility is a common result. I could feel my heart on the verge of cracking open; it felt like my chest cavity could no longer contain my heart. My limbs felt heavy and my eyes filled with tears. Desperate to keep in place the floodgate holding back my emotions, I focused intensely on the words I was hearing.

"There's another series of tests I'd like to put you through," the doctor was saying. "I'd like to do several blood tests, as well as a test to make sure you don't have any blockage in your fallopian tubes." He didn't want to give me a final diagnosis, he explained, without a complete evaluation.

Focusing on his every word, I repeated what he had said about the test for a possible blockage. "This would be a test to make sure my tubes are open?" I wanted to understand every detail of the tests he was suggesting. He remained calm and replied in a matter of fact tone, "Yes."

I nodded in recognition that I understood him and then, before I could think, the words came out. "Well, I guess it doesn't really matter if I don't have any eggs." His eyes saddened and he confirmed my statement with a final nod of his head.

It was then that I lost it and the floodgates opened. I rifled uncomfortably through my bag, desperate to find a Kleenex, as if a tissue would stop the flow of tears pouring out of my eyes. While I attempted to regain my composure, my emotions were just too much to contain. The doctor asked if I needed a moment to myself and I accepted.

I pulled myself together, checked my eyes in a pocket mirror—it was as good as it was going to get—and stepped into the hallway to head toward the front desk where I would check out. While in reality this process probably took a few minutes, it felt like an eternity. My emotions were hitting me from inside at every angle, as though there was something held captive that needed to be released. I kept looking at the front door and planning my escape to the safety of my car.

Once inside the car, the monster was out. I cried so hard I couldn't see straight. My head was pounding and everything around me looked out of focus. Still with tears flowing, I texted Tim asking if he could meet me at home. He replied instantly with, *Why, what's wrong?* All I could manage at this point was to text back: *I'll tell you at home.* He texted right back: *I'll be right there.*

Refocusing on the task at hand, I fought to keep the tears back by giving the road my full attention. I knew I needed to make it home and into Tim's arms safely. I was still in complete shock and not sure exactly how much information I had absorbed. I just knew the news wasn't good, and my dream of having our child was crumbling rapidly before me.

Tim met me as I walked through the door and without hesitation held me tight. We then sat at the kitchen table where I tried to replay the information I had been given. Tim was strong and, like I had done with the specialist, he questioned every optimistic possibility. All had reasons for not working. I could see the disappointment in Tim's eyes, yet he showed me every ounce of support I'm sure he could muster.

That afternoon, still grieving but with the shock wearing off, I turned to my current project, hoping to divert my attention from the emotions that had so overwhelmed me. I was in the final editing days of this book getting it ready for publication and, interestingly enough, I had been reworking some of the tools for becoming unstoppable that I had written about. The idea occurred to me that I could use these tools to deal with what was going on in my life now.

The title of my book immediately jumped off the page to hit me: *Becoming Unstoppable*. The question arose: *How could I possibly write a book on becoming unstoppable when I was feeling completely stopped in reaching one of my life's biggest dreams?* It was true—nothing in my life, not any of my accomplishments, honors, or awards, was as big as my dream to have a family. My book's title seemed a mockery, and my first reaction was pity and tears. But then moments later, peeking out from under my despair, I thought, *No. You are unstoppable. And you have tools!*

I continued, now writing in my journal, to coach myself: *Take all the tools you've learned from your experience over the last six years and put them to work in this current situation. No obstacle need be insurmountable. Those tools helped you heal a broken back, climb to the top of Mt. Kilimanjaro, swim Alcatraz, leap off a 30-foot pole, set audacious goals and reach them, overcome the fear of riding a bike, raise a huge sum of money for a charitable cause and become a two-time Ironman finisher!*

So, taking my own advice, that is what I began to do.

First, I acknowledged fully the current adversity in my life— *no denying this one!* I then recognized that I had choices in the matter of my diagnosed infertility. I could find new hope and new ways of thinking about reaching for my dream of motherhood, or I could roll over and let the seemingly bad news have its best shot. Not going to happen! I'm tackling it head on.

Next, I looked at the legacy statement I had written two months earlier, connecting to what my real intention and passion is about becoming a mother:

> *As a mom, I will provide a loving, compassionate, safe environment for my children to explore their true self. I will provide guidance yet remain open to their interests and desires allowing them opportunity to feel success as well as setbacks. Together with my husband Tim, I will be a role model.*

When I read my legacy statement I realized there is absolutely nothing in there that refers to me physically birthing my own child. Rather, what is important to me is nurturing, shaping, and raising a child. I wanted a baby's tiny fingers to wrap around mine, to see their tiny toes wiggle as they snuggle their sweet head into the crux of my neck. As they grow older I want to hear the patter of their footsteps and the innocent laughter of their voices. I want to watch them mature and experience all that life has to offer. I want to celebrate their victories and comfort them in their losses. Again, I was reconfirmed that none of my desires as a mother has anything to do with incubating an embryo.

This realization gave me new hope that my heart could mend, and a new way of thinking that motherhood might look different than I had originally envisioned. I knew without a doubt that I was living intentionally and living out my legacy, as this is my truth, and I could already feel future actions aligning with it.

Tim had already comforted me earlier that day with his openness to adopt. And now, reading my truth, I felt a tremendous weight lifted. Motherhood would come, it just may come wrapped in a different package than the one I expected. While the pain was still fresh, I found comfort and felt grounded by my words. I felt the full impact of Tim's earlier statement about our situation: *This doesn't define us.*

I was finding comfort in the uncomfortable. It had taken me more than 37 years to voice my true personal desires to be a wife and a mother. This was my heart's desire and life dream, and it was finally coming about. And now to find that two years later, my dream of motherhood was shattered, the pieces falling to the ground. Yet connecting to my truth provided a new level of comfort with the uncomfortable news, and I felt empowered to keep moving in my journey.

Next, I saw the word persevere and recalled the tool of thinking outside of the box. *I will persevere. My eye is on the ball—I will be a mother.* I felt my strength as I continued to journal: *I will do everything possible to create a child with my husband. I will not give up hope of our original dream. I will also be wise and create a plan, realizing that in the game of life, a ball may be passed to me unexpectedly. I will work to keep the ball in play. Thus, my goal is inevitable.*

I decided right then and there I was not going to become a statistic that fertility specialists quote to their patients. I was not going to let the statistic of "less than 5%" scare me. I was connected to my passion and knew what I wanted in life.

By this point I was so uplifted and hopeful, there was no doubt in my mind that a powerful intrinsic motivator lay within my legacy statement. Accessing all my tools, my drive had become stronger than any obstacle before me.

In perfect timing, Tim walked through the door, and I ended my journal entry and closed the draft of my book. My emotions had drained me, leaving me exhausted. Yet at the same time, I felt an empowering sense of confidence and peace. Tim and I lay down for a nap and were joined by Kingston, whose sensitivity in the moment to what we were both feeling was touching. It was a powerful moment, the three of us together. This was our family...for now. But the future is full of possibility—and new hope—knowing that in my heart I am *Unstoppable.*

# ABOUT THE AUTHOR

 Kristy Bidwill is a business professional, certified sports life coach, and athlete. Growing up in a life filled with competitive sports gave Kristy the discipline and ambition to pursue her dreams. She attributes living a life of intention and purpose to her ongoing love of sports and the knowledge she has gained.

As founder and owner of Game Time Coaching, a company dedicated to helping individuals and teams elevate their game through the language of sports, she has committed her career to serving others in achieving the same results she has experienced personally. Whether she is working with athletes or executives, her goal is to give them the plays necessary to reach levels they never thought possible, finding a balance of optimal performance in both their personal and professional lives. With a strong passion for making a difference, Kristy works with for-profit and nonprofit organizations alike to provide inspiration and motivation through various speaking and training opportunities.

Kristy has been recognized as a dynamic leader receiving many awards throughout her career. Among the most notable, she was named *Marketer of the Year in 2005;* and in 2009, she was awarded the Phoenix Business Journal's *Volunteer Spirit Award* as well as being named to the publication's *Forty Under 40* list.

Prior to her work as a coach and speaker, Kristy was a partner at an international architectural, engineering, and planning firm. As a Principal with more than 17 years' experience in the industry, she led their business development efforts throughout the Southwest and oversaw marketing and public relations.

Kristy's competitive sports career has covered the gamut. She was a competitive gymnast and later coach; a competitive college cheerleader, ranking 7th in the country; a first-degree black belt and two-time Junior Olympic medal holder in Tae Kwon Do. She has also swum Alcatraz, led a blind man to the summit of Mt. Kilimanjaro, completed 10 marathons, and is a two-time Ironman.

Born and raised in Kansas, Kristy moved to Phoenix, Arizona in 1996 after graduating from Kansas State University with a business degree. She now lives a life of passion and purpose with her husband, Tim and their Rhodesian Ridgeback, Kingston.

You can learn more about Kristy and Game Time Coaching by visiting www.GameTimeCoaching.com. Elevate Your Game!

# GAME | TIME
## COACHING

Do you ever find yourself wanting more out of life even though to most you have it all? You are successful, ambitious and live a full life. On paper you appear to be living the dream, yet inside there is a lingering feeling as though you are missing a key element and cannot pinpoint it. Or maybe you know exactly what is missing, yet you have struggled to overcome it on your own. Perhaps you have tried countless programs, coaching, and consultants and read more books than your home library can hold. Let us introduce you to a whole new game...

This is where Game Time Coaching differs from anything you've experienced before. Through the language of sports, you will find new perspective and learn new skills to create solutions leading you to life of sustainable optimal performance. You will walk away with the tools to generate life changing game plays giving you the competitive edge to winning seasons in every aspect of your life.

Whether you are an executive at the top of your career or one trying to climb the corporate ladder, whether you are an amateur athlete or a professional, a leader of a team looking to make a profound impact in your industry, an athletic coach looking to achieve a memorable feat, or simply an individual in the midst of transition, Game Time Coaching can help.

Our approach to coaching is 100% customized to each individual and/or team. We take a client driven approach rather than program driven. The end result equips you with a playbook of skills in which you will personalize, build upon and continually implement in all areas of your life. Through the use of your new playbook, you will write your own unique competitive edge that makes the difference between a winning and losing season. No two playbooks will ever be the same.

Small changes can make big differences.

www.GameTimeCoaching.com